Mythological Woman

MYTHOLOGICAL WOMAN

Contemporary Reflections on Ancient Religious Stories

Denise Lardner Carmody

CROSSROAD · NEW YORK

For Joan Fiege

1992
The Crossroad Publishing Company
370 Lexington Avenue, New York, NY 10017

Library of Congress Cataloging-in-Publication Data

Carmody, Denise Lardner, 1935–
    Mythological woman : contemporary reflections on ancient
religious stories / Denise Lardner Carmody.
        p.   cm.
    Includes bibliographical references.
    ISBN 0-8245-1217-0 (pbk.)
    1. Women   and   religion. 2. Women—
Mythology.   I. Title.
    BL458.C35 1992   92-26086
    291.2'114—dc20   CIP

Contents

Preface

This book is my third collection of reflections on texts and traditions influential in the development of religious views of women. Its focus is mythological materials. From prehistoric and historic Europe, Asian cultures, Near Eastern cultures, and recent oral cultures I have selected stories about women or femininity that I find charged with more than rational significance. To suggest their implications for present-day feminists, men as well as women, I have first explained the context in which they arose and then reflected on the lessons, both timeless and contemporary, that I find them to carry. The result, I hope, is a provocative argument that female nature has always stimulated impressive stories grounding the specific humanity of women in the sacredness of the divine. How important readers find this argument to be will probably depend on their estimate of how greatly present-day women feel profaned, or how crucial it is to see the humanity of women as equal to that of men—neither more exalted nor more lowly.

My thanks to Frank Oveis of the Crossroad Publishing Company, to the many feminist scholars now laboring to assess the riches of the religions' views of women, and to my husband John Carmody.

1

Introduction

MYTH

I begin with an image from *Maryknoll*, a monthly magazine edited by the Maryknoll missionaries. In a photo meditation for the feast of the Assumption of the Virgin Mary into heaven, Joseph R. Veneroso, M.M., writes beside a picture of a lovely woman from Bangladesh: "Her body, perfect temple of God, represents all the universe. The barrier between heaven and earth crumbles at her word."[1] The context is the complex of mysteries associated with Mary, which includes not only her Assumption into heaven but also her agreement to the Incarnation at the Annunciation. Trading on millennia during which the body of woman was an image of the earth, Christian tradition and the author of this meditation see in woman's yes to divine or male overtures the key to fertility, whether physical or spiritual. Knowingly or not, the author is dealing in myth. For weal, in this case, or woe, in many other cases, women continue to be the subjects of a considerable mythology. My interest in this book is to reflect on the history of such mythology in the world religions.

But what is "myth"? This word, whose basic etymological significance is "tale," "speech," or "story," has been widely bandied about in recent religious studies. Many scholars find in religious myths an effort to express something heavenly in earthly garb, something eternal in temporal terms. One catches part of the conversation that historians of religions have been conducting about mythology in the following excerpt from an orientational essay by Mircea Eliade, perhaps the most important figure in the rise of scholarly analysis of religious myths.

All the mythology that is accessible to us in a significant state of conservation contains not only a beginning but also an end, bounded by the final manifestations of the Supernatural Beings, the Heroes or the Ancestors. So this primordial sacred history, formed by the body of significant myths, is fundamental, for it explains and justifies at the same time the existence of the world, of man [humanity], and of society. This is why myth is considered both a *true story*—because it tells how real things have come to be—and the exemplary model of and justification for the activities of man. One understands what one is—mortal and sexual—and one assumes this condition because myths tell how death and sexuality made their appearance in the world. One engages in a certain type of hunting or agriculture because myths tell how the enculturating Heroes revealed these techniques to one's ancestors.[2]

Several comments may be helpful. First, Eliade is speaking about the overall function of myths in world history—how most if not all societies have oriented themselves through guiding stories. He is not limiting himself to Christian myths, and he is not dealing with the question of whether modern human beings have outgrown mythology. Second, the focus is myths of origin, which many scholars consider the most important or influential. Eliade is pointing out that, influential as myths of origin are, they never occur in isolation. Always there are enough references to aspects of present existence and patterns of future consummation to suggest a sacred history—a story of how what is most important about the world and human beings began, came to its present condition, and will finish.

Third, this sacred story is characteristically the doing of supernatural beings. Call them Heroes or Ancestors or gods, they bear the major responsibility for why the world is as it is, why the human condition is as it is. Thus there is something intrinsically mysterious about religious mythology. Though the tales about the origin of the world and the end of the world offer valuable information, they remain more pregnant than human beings can know. For the makers of the world stand on a different plane from human beings. They are gods or giants, whom human beings can never comprehend fully.

Fourth, human beings consider their sacred tales true information or revelation about how reality is constructed, and they use such information to fashion models for their own conduct. The myths are exemplary tales, showing human beings how to live. They have vast existential implications. Inasmuch as meaning, and so culture, depends on the images that people carry of how they ought to live, what it means to be an authentic man or woman, the myths that supply such meaning have a great say in the rise and development of human cultures.

Finally, the myths stress mortality and sexuality. In other places Eliade has shown the link between these two forces, explaining in rich detail humanity's constant wonder about them. Here it suffices to note that myths are the main way that human beings have reconciled themselves to the necessity that they die and that sexuality spotlights both a natural strategy for holding mortality at bay and a primary wonder of the human condition: the differences between men and women.

Traditionally, then, human beings the world over have used their myths (which they indwelt through elaborate rituals) to explain their situation. They have drawn on the stories of how the world began, how significant aspects of their culture came into place, why living things die, what sexuality implies, and how the cosmos will end, to make their way through time. Without myths, they would not have been human. As far as we know, animals have no reflective hold on their situations, follow no exemplary stories, and do not comfort themselves with tales of the beginning and the end. Mythology is a specifically human phenomenon.

It follows that myths have shaped the experiences of all significant groups of human beings throughout history. Not only Greeks and Chinese, Christians and Muslims, Siberians and denizens of Tierra del Fuego, but also old people and children, kings and commoners, healthy people and sick people have set their course by mythical stars.

Equally, it follows that men and women have understood themselves through the myths regnant in their cultures. Moreover, this understanding has been mutual, bipolar. Men have defined who they were through the exemplary stories of their people, and women have commented on masculinity using those stories. Women have defined who they were through the relevant myths of their culture, and men have commented on femininity in the same coin. Inevitably, the stories and so the self-understandings of men and women have overlapped, conflicted, and supported one another. Inevitably, they have been both symmetrical and asymmetrical.

Men and women are ordered to one another. Procreation requires their minimal cooperation. The bisexual character of the human race has ensured that human culture would be both male and female. Even if one sex has been in the political ascendancy, the other has commented, reinterpreted, defended, and promoted itself from the underside, reactively. Power has been covert as well as overt, a matter of subtle persuasion as well as brute force. Women have had as much say in the construction of meaning as men, because perforce meaning, culture, has contained both voices, both reports on what being human entails.

The pattern throughout recorded history, however, has been for cultures to be patriarchal—ruled in official matters by men. Perhaps there were exceptions to this pattern in prehistoric cultures, and some cultures of the historical era (the period since the development of written records) seem to have been relatively egalitarian. On the whole, though, men's has been the official interpretative voice and women's the voice rejoining, if not debunking.

For our topic, then, the mythical understanding of women appears as something much worked over by men. Most of the records in which we can study the images of women in cultures of the past were probably composed by men and reflected men's ideas. We have to assume that these ideas influenced women greatly, but we cannot assume that women swallowed whole everything that the official myths presented to them, let alone everything that men imposed on them. As feminist studies of the past develop, we find more and more evidence that women regularly fashioned subcultures at some variance from the official cultures ruled by male poets, priests, kings, teachers, generals, politicians, and other mavens.

Still, the basic asymmetry that appears in the traditional mythology of women stems from the official, male-dominated culture and is highly suggestive. Officially, women are not as human as men. This thesis, so regularly propounded in traditional cultures, ramifies in many different directions. For present purposes, two directions are especially significant. First, women are a secondary or derivative instance of humanity, and so somehow defective, less authoritative. It makes no sense, then, for women to claim rule or authority in any sphere not exclusively their own. Second, women do not exist on the same level as men. They are either more degraded or more exalted. Men attribute to women the worst corruption and the highest sanctity. Women live at the peaks and the valleys. Men inhabit the plains of ordinary, normal, everyday humanity—the zone that inevitably commands 80 percent of people's energy and loyalty.

Mythical woman is therefore hellish and heavenly beyond her male counterpart. She represents the extremes more than he, while he represents the medians. One of my interests in this book is musing about what this asymmetrical understanding of the sexes has tended to mean throughout religious history. These stories, which human beings have indwelt, sung, danced, and used as the principal language through which they talked to themselves about who they were, have indeed stressed the otherness of women more than their sameness with men. Given such stories, how have women, and men, configured the place of women in the history of salvation, the economy of the divine-human effort to move humanity from sin to grace, from self-destructiveness to creativity, from sickness to health? Assuming that the crux of culture, the most basic intent of humanity's efforts to discover or create meaning, is the understanding of human destiny, how have women figured in this intent and the results it has generated?

Certainly, one cannot separate intuitions of human destiny from images and intuitions of human origin. The end and the beginning are married, joined for richer or poorer. But in this study destiny—where we are going or may hope to go—intrigues me more. Where could women hope to go, what roles could women play, and what contributions could women make to the overall going of humankind? If wisdom was the key to going well, what were the relevant feminine wisdoms? If love was the engine or energy, what were the relevant feminine loves? By placing questions such as these in the background of the texts on which I reflect, I hope to suggest how contemporary women, and men, may read the history of their mythical foremothers and foresisters most profitably.

THIS BOOK

The foremothers and foresisters relevant to this project are legion—one cannot even imagine all their faces and names. For the fact seems to be that in traditional, premodern cultures, all women, and men, were mythologized to a significant degree. The basic pattern of traditional societies was that heavenly archetypes served as the models for earthly behavior and selfunderstanding. The culture hero not only brought the gift of farming or blacksmithing, he also set the standards and defined the role for human farmers and blacksmiths. The Buffalo Maiden not only brought the gift of the animal that gave the tribe food and clothing, her bearing became the standard, the ideal, for the earthly woman contemplating her.

In one sense, then, what engages us in this book is encyclopedic. Before the time when supposedly "enlightened" human beings set about debunking myths (persuading people that myths were not true but false tales, much inferior to modern science), virtually all men and women structured their worlds in terms of what the stories most central in their cultures told them about the origins of the cosmos and the roles of men and women. All traditional human lives were mythical, because all traditional women and men thought that existence in time was a pale but genuine reflection of the sacred, fully real existence of the gods in heaven. What went on below was a miniature of, a participation in, the full-blown experience of living that divine females and males carried out on high.

Still, it makes sense to focus on the central tales of different traditional cultures, thinking that the stories apparently at the heart of their sense of ultimate reality were the most influential in determining how traditional men and women lived. Since we are studying the mythical forces most significant for women, we focus on the stories of paradigmatic females. We thus frequently find ourselves concerned with great goddesses—paradigmatic females thought crucial to the functioning of the cosmos.

Again and again the first significance of these females, apparent in the images dominating the tales about them, is their fertility. They bring forth life. As mother earth, or the cosmic source of offspring, they enable creation to ward off death, destruction, sterility, and the other expressions of contingency, nondivinity. This raises philosophical questions, of course, because the great goddesses also preside over death, making it also an aspect of ultimate reality. How can divinity be the source of both life and death? Different traditional cultures have handled the cluster of paradoxes implied in this question in different ways, but a regular result of their reflections has been the symbolic rule of female divinities over both life and death.

In symbolism that is nearly constant among premodern peoples, the divine female has been the one from whom life issued and to whom life returned. The cosmic womb has pushed life forth but also received it back. In the spring life came forth from mother earth, but in the fall it returned to mother earth. Father sky played an important role, supplying fertilizing sun and rain, but birth, life, and death remained the province of mother earth. The grasses were her hair. The stones were her bones. To cut into her bosom by plowing was a serious, perhaps impious venture. To work the ore in her innards called for a special asceticism and holiness. One may laugh at the simplicity of this conception, but one has also to admire its elegance. It made sense of the round of births and deaths, the succession of generations, the cycles of nature, the waxing and waning of the moon, the interconnectedness of all mortal things (the dead fertilize the earth, giving the living nourishment).

We begin our reflections on the mythical views of femininity that the stable traditional understandings of life and death tended to generate by dealing with the primordial female, or Great Goddess, of Old Europe. As archaeologists have documented with increasing completeness, from the earliest records of prehistoric Europe we find a fascination with fertility and death. Regularly this fascination focuses on figurines of females, careful study of which reveals that prehistoric Europeans tended to give a feminine form to the powers most responsible for their fate. Such prehistoric human beings were complex, so the symbolisms they developed were not simple. Nonetheless, by studying some recent work on the artifacts of Old Europe, we can gain a good foundation for our study of how cultures the world over have mythologized women.

Classical Greece is our second stop. There we find a well-articulated mythology that spread feminine qualities or potential across a rich span of goddesses. Because the mythology of classical Greece became a wellspring of European culture, influential long after the supposed conversion of Europe to Christianity, goddesses such as Hera and Artemis are familiar to many Western readers. In other traditional European cultures, the pantheon of goddesses might be equally rich, but it was not so well organized. So, our foray into classical Greek mythology can stand bail for what we might find, were we to investigate Roman, Celtic, Slavic, or Germanic mythical depictions of femininity.

Having begun with European sources, we move to their Asian equivalents. In India and China, the two great basins of Asian culture, goddesses were the centerpieces of rich mythologies in which women found models to contemplate, and men found paradigms to study. Both Hindus and Buddhists inherited centuries' worth of Indian imaginings about the ways of males and females, the forces of life and death. Hindus made more of goddesses than Buddhists did, because the Buddha debunked the popular divinities of his day, but the heavenly or eternal feminine cropped up in Buddhism as well, for example, in the descriptions of holy Wisdom, the vision from nirvana, the far side of human existence. In East Asia, Buddhism developed true mother goddesses such as Kuan-yin, to whom millions of Chinese have looked for mercy, and Tara, the equivalent Madonna of Tibet. Naturally, neither of these figures was the only source for defining what femininity meant in traditional China or Tibet, but in both cases we learn a great deal by studying the most popular goddesses. Analogously, we learn a great deal by studying Amaterasu, the sun goddess of Japan.

The religions that arose in the ancient Near East also fashioned significant goddesses, though by the time that Judaism, Christianity, and Islam came on the scene, femininity had come under a cloud, because these religions were leery of fertility. The God supposedly revealed to Abraham, further clarified in Jesus, and described definitively in the Qur'an was a single God, fully spiritual, and quite male. He did not truck with women's ways, though in the final analysis one can find stereotypically feminine traits in his person, and he stood beyond the natural world, free of its patterns of life and death, fertility and mortality.

By studying how the divine feminine appeared in the ancient Near East outside the orbit of the prophetic, biblical religions, and then by considering where femininity continued to claim psychic space in traditional Judaism, Christianity, and Islam, we gain further insight into the messages that traditional women received. As well, we prepare ourselves to deal with the question of where Jewish, Christian, and Muslim women find themselves

today, in cultures supposedly postmodern but often still structured by powerful myths.

Our final stop is the myths of recent oral peoples such as
Native Americans, traditional Africans, and traditional Australians. They are "recent" oral peoples in that their traditional
cultures have persisted into the twentieth century. They clearly
display a great variety of myths, rituals, and theologies. For our
purposes, however, which are mainly to note how religions not
tied to written texts have tended to imagine sacred femininity,
it is convenient to consider them together.

The conclusions to which we come, after our survey, will be
modest, because by the end it will be clear how vast a tract of
history and psychology we have surveyed. Perforce we shall have
concentrated on only a small sample of the exemplary materials
relevant to our topic. The best consequence of realizing this
would be for readers to continue on their own, examining many
more artifacts and texts.

As was true with my previous books on the sources of our
conceptions of sacred femininity,[3] my procedure will be to provide a focus for study, explain the context in which the focus
(the given artifact or text) appears, and then reflect on the
significance that it might bear for contemporary readers. In other
words, first we consider the datum on its own terms, then we
ask what it could mean for us today.

In taking such a second step, I make explicit what I consider
the second half of the hermeneutical circle. This circle is the
round of interactions necessary to interpret a text or other source
of information. The first half is to get the text in focus on its
own terms, to situate it historically, understand what it assumed
and was trying to say. The second half is to make what it was
trying to say one's own, to find what, if any, permanent validity
it carries. Implied in this second movement is a willingness to
engage one's present consciousness with the text.

Taken to heart, such a willingness both honors the text as a
possible source of wisdom-for-me and pressures me to compare
my assumptions, needs, and hopes with those shaping it. So the

circle can be—and should be—traveled more than once. The richer the text, the more frequent the goings and comings between reader and source. Ideally dialogue gets under way, and eventually the text and the interpreter become contemporaries. The text lives in the interpreter's present, while the interpreter journeys back to the time of text. Only the most accomplished scholars become full contemporaries of their texts, but even amateurs can expand their horizons significantly by taking to heart ancient texts, specimens of foreign or even alien cultures.

I hope to make the texts with which we deal sufficiently beautiful to invite even the casual reader to take them to heart. They suggest much of the story of how human beings have thought about being female, and though that story includes immense suffering, it has moments of beauty so surpassing that both sexes need to hear it well.

2

Old Europe and Classical Greece

CHEVRON AND V SYMBOLS

Early in Marija Gimbutas's well-illustrated work *The Language of the Goddess*, we find representations of pieces of ivory from the Upper Paleolithic period of Old Europe. Archaeologists estimate that these pieces, found at Mezin, in the upper Desna basin of the Ukraine, come from the period 18,000–15,000 B.C. Their distinctive feature is V-shaped incisions. In some cases the incisions remain the only decoration, making the piece of ivory an abstract work of art. In other cases the incisions adorn pieces carved to resemble waterbirds. The waterbirds have an anthropomorphic quality, but they remain recognizably birds. In describing several specimens from the find at Mezin, Gimbutas writes: "Abstract form and symbolic decoration combine in these upper Paleolithic ivory figurines of anthropomorphized waterbirds incised with V's and chevrons (multiple V's). The decorations of the figure on the right [her book provides a series of specimens] serve to emphasize her pubic triangle, and thus her divine generative function."[1]

Though Gimbutas spreads descriptions such as this throughout her work, speaking in the dispassionate tone of the accomplished scientist, she allows herself more emotion in her introduction:

The purpose of this book is to present the pictorial script for the religion of the Old European Great Goddess, consisting of signs, symbols, and images of divinities. These are our primary sources for reconstructing this prehistoric scene and are vital to any true understanding of Western religion and mythology.

Some twenty years ago when I first started to question the meaning of the signs and design patterns that appeared repeatedly on the cult objects and painted pottery of Neolithic Europe, they struck me as being pieces of a gigantic jigsaw puzzle—two-thirds of which was missing. As I worked at its completion, the main themes of Old European ideology emerged, primarily through analysis of the symbols and images and discovery of their intrinsic order. They represent the grammar and syntax of a kind of meta-language by which an entire constellation of meanings is transmitted. They reveal the basic world-view of Old European (pre-Indo-European) culture.

. . . What is striking is not the metamorphosis of the symbols over the millennia but rather the continuity from Paleolithic times on. The major aspects of the Goddess of the Neolithic—the birth-giver portrayed in a naturalistic birth-giving pose; the fertility-giver influencing growth and multiplication, portrayed as a pregnant nude; the life or nourishment-giver and protectress, portrayed as a bird-woman with breasts and protruding buttocks; and the death-wielder as a stiff nude (bone)—can all be traced back to the period when the first sculptures of bones, ivory, or stone appeared, around 25,000 B.C., and their symbols—vulvas, triangles, breasts, chevrons, zig-zags, meanders, cupmarks—to an even earlier time. The main theme of Goddess symbolism is the mystery of birth and death and the renewal of life, not only human but all life on earth and indeed in the whole cosmos.[2]

So a piece of ivory incised with V's is our first artifact. We begin our study of mythical woman with data more than 25,000 years old. Interestingly, these data are already abstract. The figurines are not portraits of individual women. They do not represent Eva or Marie. Neither do they represent particular waterbirds, whether tamed or wild. The associations they brought to the then-contemporary mind were universal. They invited Paleolithic people to contemplate the wonders of life and death, the mysterious processes of coming into being and passing away.

The waterbird had connotations of moisture and air useful for suggesting the cosmic dimensions of fertility. The V's and chevrons represented specifically human femininity and fertility. Brilliantly, the simple V that called to mind the human vulva epitomized the locale and processes of human conception, gestation, and birth. The wonder of human procreation could be condensed in a fleeting reference to the female genitalia. Whereas breasts suggested nourishment of life already produced, the chevrons suggested the very origins of life. Large buttocks might symbolize an amplitude of vitality or sexuality, but once again, the chevrons pointed to the quintessential feature. Life emerged from the wombs of women. How life became planted in the wombs of women could be unclear, though it was obvious that copulation with men played a role. But the processes of conception and gestation remained hidden. Even women who had conceived, carried, and given birth to numerous children could not see these processes or explain life's origins.

When women complain that they are considered sex objects, they lament a failure of personalism. They feel they are being considered generic sources of pleasure or fertility, rather than distinct individuals. The abstract art of the Upper Paleolithic is a salutary reminder that personalism is a recent, perhaps only a modern, phenomenon. Naturally, we should not conclude that this abstract art meant that no Paleolithic women were treated as individuals. But the fact remains that the predominant interest was the generic capacity of females to give birth. Giving pleasure or nourishment was secondary to giving birth. Being a distinct individual came in a poor third. Birth, and so life, was the great treasure of Paleolithic cultures. Only a little reflection suggests why.

At the most, the average span of life 25,000 years ago was about half what it is for contemporary Westerners. People who reached fifty were extraordinary. Infant mortality was high. Many women died in childbirth. People had few ways to store food for more than several months. Hunting and gathering was a precarious way to sustain a living. Nature so dominated human strengths that storms, earthquakes, seasons of unusual heat, drought, flood, or even steady rain could imperil existence. The only bulwark against extinction was the fertility of women. As food and shelter were to daily survival, so procreation was to the ongoing survival of the tribe. Women who were not fertile failed their raison d'être. The reason for women to be was off-spring. The center of a woman's significance was the center of her body, the V marking the spot of her fertility.

If this was the message broadcast to women through millennia of prehistory, how did it mold the traditional female psyche? Though individuals could depart from stock criteria of self-worth, most traditional women were bound to make motherhood the center of their lives. Infertile women would lament their misfortune, petitioning the Goddess for a change of fortune. Fertile women would consider the pangs of childbirth and the burdens of caring for children a fair price for their sense of satisfaction and fulfillment, having become what they were made to be through their progeny. Only when cultures became more sophisticated did the role of wife swell to rival that of mother. For the majority of human generations, to be born female has meant being considered a mother, potential or actual.

Traditionally, women bound their children to them for political purposes, using their offspring as markers in the games they had to play with men. The more loyal their children were, especially their sons, the more power women had. Women also instructed other women in the traditional female arts of healing, preparing food, caring for children, pleasing men, and offering the quirky wisdoms of people freed (by sitting on the margins of power) to speak up when the leaders had no clothes. But the first thing that women did was provide children. The central focus of traditional female meaning was obstetrical. Have contemporary women underestimated this legacy from the distant, long-standing past?

Yes and no, observation and intuition tell me. No, women continue to be oriented to children. The gentleness, intimacy, patience, drama, awareness, and other qualities that one associates with the skillful, loving, dedicated mother continue to play a large role in women's psyches. The majority of women continue to want marriage and motherhood. The dossier of the "complete" woman continues to have a large space for the names and accomplishments of her children.

But yes, contemporary women tend to underappreciate the past, when providing offspring to the tribe was crucially important, in large part because humanity's problem today is not underpopulation but overpopulation. Today we need to curb fertility more than ensure it. Certainly, there is a grand debate about the connection between the procreative and the personal, even romantic, aspects of sexual congress, but in most of the developed world the spotlight has shifted to personal issues. One sees this in the American discussion of abortion. The major issue, in the eyes of many advocates of women's rights, is the ability to control one's fertility: the right to choose. The objective rights of the tribe to secure offspring from women's fertility are far down the list of considerations, if indeed they appear at all.

What does it mean that many individual women no longer feel the pressure to produce children for the common good, the general survival? On the one hand, it means a blessed freedom from generic responsibilities that could be overwhelming and dehumanizing. On the other hand, it means dangers of reducing children to instruments of their parents' pleasure and ignoring the objective messages built into sexual differentiation.

The fact is that the pubic V of women continues to signify volumes about the construction of reality. The fact is that fertility, however domesticated and apparently commonplace, continues to tell those with eyes to see that life is sacred. The majority of parents, men as well as women, greet the appearance of a child as an inexplicable wonder. Even the sophisticated, the highly secularized, often confess that seeing their newborn "blew them away." For many women the experience of giving birth is ecstatic. Despite the pain, something so extraordinary occurs that part of them is gripped by awe.

The same for many fathers upon first holding their new little child, son or daughter. Many marvel that so tiny a bundle could draw from them such depths of emotion, so much joy and tenderness. Paleolithic counselors might well smile and suggest that these apparently private, personalist reactions depend on the larger picture of humanity's ancient struggle to survive. Beyond the satisfaction of seeing one's own genes replicated lies a gratitude and sense of completion: one has increased, multiplied, been fruitful, contributed one's mite to the survival of the race. One has been privileged to participate in the primordial struggle of humankind to outwit disease, death, and its own evils for another generation.

In the ideal case, some perception of this cosmic dimension of procreation would bring both women and men to a sense of stewardship. Instead of asking, querulously, "What has posterity ever done for me?" thoughtful adults would experience their children as a call to secure the earth for another generation—to keep its war making in check, its ecology viable. Indeed, in the chevrons of Paleolithic women lies an ecological imperative. Whether they realize it or not, "ecofeminists" fiercely determined to protect the maternal earth are honoring the objective significance of their distant foremothers, even as they hoist the load of humanity's future.

THE STIFF WHITE LADY

The great proliferation of prehistoric artifacts dealing with a sacral femininity broadcasts loud and clear that from the time human beings began to contemplate life and death, they wondered about women. It is significant, though, that many Paleolithic, Mesolithic, and Neolithic figurines do not stress fertility. Female figures are always marked by attention to genitalia, breasts, or buttocks, but some are not fat, round, obviously overflowing with fertility. In fact, a distinctive genus of artifacts presents stiff, elongated female figures. In some instructive cases, these "white ladies" appear to link femininity with death.

Gimbutas says of such stiff white ladies:

> A distinct stereotype in figurine art is the nude with folded or extended arms, a supernatural vulva, a long neck, and no face, or with a masked head and polos or diadem. The media are marble, alabaster, amber, light-colored stone, bone, and some-times clay. The light color is the color of bone—that is, of death. The anthropomorphic female Death of European folklore to this day is imagined as tall, bony-legged, and dressed in white. No doubt she is inherited from the Old European substratum when death was bone white, not black like the terrifying Indo-Euro-pean male god of death and the underworld. Made of bone, ivory, or reindeer antler; schematized stiff nudes with arms folded or pressed to the sides, a large pubic triangle, and tapering legs appear in the Upper Paleolithic. They are categorically different from the famous Willendorf-Lespugue type with large breasts, belly, and buttocks, and from the Sireuil-Tursac type representing birth-giving.[3]

As even a cursory reading of Gimbutas's large book reveals, the goddesses of Old Europe gathered to themselves a great many associations. Birds, snakes, deer, bears, and rams could represent or accompany the Old European Goddess. Streams brought her to mind, but so did particular numbers, such as three and two, and particular crafts, such as spinning, weaving, and making music. The majority of these associations were positive, in the sense that they accompanied her presidency over birth, life, and fertility. But another group of animals associated her with death: vultures, owls, boars, and dogs. Also, the egg that could repre-sent her, like her womb, suggested a tomb—a place of return to the uterine earth, perhaps as a way station to another round of existence.

Prehistoric peoples had to pay close attention to the cycles of nature. Their hunting and gathering depended on a good knowledge of natural rhythms, the times when animals migrated or hibernated, where and when useful herbs or berries were likely to appear. Indeed, it seems likely that the earliest efforts at computation focused on the cycles of nature and that observation of the heavens, as well as the earth, became a stimulus to mathematics.[4]

In addition, it took millennia for human beings to differentiate their powers to *abstract* (from individual material items) and correlate them knowingly with their powers to *imagine* (concrete material forms). What we now blithely call "intellect" and "imagination" were fused until relatively recently (until the rise of classical philosophy in Greece, about 2,500 years ago).[5] So it was natural for people reflecting on death and its relations with life to see connotations and implications in many different directions. It was natural not only to imagine the tomb as a womb but to associate with the womb-bearing sacred female the vulture or the howling dog, who also figured in the human experience of death.

Thus the stiff white lady appears in the midst of a rich field of long-standing associations. She is white because the most striking feature of the person long-dead is the skeleton—the reduction to an essence of bone. In addition to burying corpses, prehistoric peoples might leave them exposed, to be hurried on their way back into the pool of raw materials by vultures or dogs. The experience of death could cut two ways, psychologically. People might show their care for the departed by laying them tenderly in the womb of the telluric mother, or they might feel polluted by the experience of death and so want to distance the corpse from the human community. In this second case they might tell themselves that the true identity of their beloved mother or child (now snatched from them) lay in its breath, its vital spirit. With that spirit gone, it no longer was the one who had nursed her children so tenderly or brought light to his parents' eyes.

Whether coming as a black male figure, out of the depths of the Indo-European speculations about death, or as a stiff white lady, born of Old European meditations on bone, death was polluting because it threatened life, and so everything beautiful and lovable. Sickness was the pathway to death, so sickness too was polluting. Blood flowed when death came violently, so blood appeared polluting. Women flowed with blood each month, so how should one estimate women's sacredness? How could the same being bring forth the holiest thing, new life, and yet stand so close to death, the worst evil?

The ambivalence toward women that we find in all patriarchal cultures has deep historical, symbolic, and psychological roots such as these. It is no accident that the Goddess of Old Europe is both the round, fertile, almost jolly source of life and the stiff, elongated, severe bringer of death. In the latter form, her arms stay close to her sides, because human beings do not want to embrace her or imagine her as embracing them. To enter her embrace is horrifying. She is bony-legged because she is so well represented by bone. Death is a formidable kind of being, but not the attractive, generous, well-padded kind conducive to generation.

If we were engaged in a wholesale study of death, across a great variety of cultures, both ancient and modern, we would have to give equal weight to the male symbols, or their lack, that our study turned up. Here, where our interest is how women have fared in the mythic imagination of the species, we may concentrate on symbols, such as the stiff white lady, that make death a formidable female force. What ought present-day women and men to make of the stiff white lady? What can it alert us to see in the perception and treatment of women?

It may surprise us to find that older peoples feminized death. The associations between women and birth are so strong and obvious that sometimes it seems only logical to dichotomize culture into a feminine zone that pivots on life and a masculine zone that pivots on death. Women give birth, gather food from plants, prepare food, are the main nurses, care for children and, recently, dominate the ranks of those protesting against military or ecological destructiveness. Women live longer than men, seem to care more about bodily things, experience in their bodies an alternation of waxing and waning that calls to mind not only the alternations of the moon but also nature's cycles of full and fallow, life and death. "Mother" nature, "mother" earth, and even "mother" church trade on this association of women with birth and life.

Men are most of the soldiers, as they have been most of the hunters. Men perpetrate most of the violent crimes and seem more likely than women to indulge in death-defying pursuits, to live on the edge of danger (risking different kinds of death, economic or spiritual, as well as physical), to gamble as though life were not precious. Women tend to feel that life is more precious to them than to men because they have borne it in the womb and cared for it in its most vulnerable moments. Thus the Pietà is a classical expression of women's associations with death: a woman, the Mother of God, receives back the child that a cruel world has killed before his time.

So it is salutary for women to think about their natural associations with death, as well as life. It is challenging to think that death is also a womb and that men can fear sexual, political, or economic subordination or surrender to women as a kind of death. Perhaps the stiffness of the white lady is another clue to a profitable contemplation. Perhaps the different ways that culture, and women themselves, conspire to make femininity hard, rigid, and even frigid are potent expressions of what is most frightening in human potential. The conservatives who lament the entry of women into the military or business or the ministry have few arguments likely to persuade people convinced that women are as fully human as men. However, perhaps the best of such conservatives have instructive fears or even intuitions. Without capitulating to their sexism, we ought to listen to their fears.

In the best cases, they worry that women will become hard, and so that home life or church life will lose something precious. They worry that women will get caught in the rush of worldly doing, worldly dealing with power, and they sense, at a primordial level, that this rush is headlong, lemminglike, toward death.

There is no lasting, spiritual life in worldly affairs. Worldly affairs are ephemeral, when they are not deliberately destructive. Worldly affairs count out winners and losers, like judges passing sentence on who will live and who will die. They destroy the hope for a continuing symbiosis with the great mother, the nature quintessentially fruitful and nurturing.

It is foolish to think that one might legislate women's removal from such worldly activity, but perhaps not foolish to hope that women themselves, free of compulsion either to join or to stay apart from secular affairs, will think carefully about the rules of the games, the operations, the institutions that they are joining. How can they recognize the pressures to become or represent the stiff white lady? How can they distinguish between the feminine aspects of death that are natural, and so part of a bone-deep wisdom about the passingness of everything human, its return to the womb of mother earth, and the lamentable appearances in the female psyche of aberrant aspects previously considered male, such as violence and ruthless competition? In a word, present-day feminists, female or male, would be wise not to ignore the connections among frigidity, death, and secularization. When they see women locking their arms at their sides, freezing their psyches, unwilling or unable to embrace life warmly, they should wonder about the losses that modernization can bring.

HERA

In her quite personal study of goddesses of classical Greece, Christine Downing comes to Hera while in the midst of a divorce. She notes the traditions that suggest Hera's independence of Zeus, prior to their marriage, and Hera's growth to the status of a sacred symbol for all the stages of a woman's life, all the feminine aspects of divine fertility and care for creation.

The Orphic hymn to Hera invokes her thus: "You are ensconced in darksome hollows, and airy is your form, O Hera, queen of all, the blessed consort of Zeus. You send soft breezes to mortals, such as nourish the soul, and, O mother of rains, you nurture the winds and give birth to all. Without you there is neither life nor growth: and, mixed as you are in the air we venerate, you partake of all, and of all you are queen and mistress. You toss and turn with the rushing wind. May you, O blessed goddess, and many-named queen of all, come with kindness and joy on your lovely face." The Hera of cult was worshiped by all women and was pertinent to every stage of a woman's life. She was Hera Parthenos, Hera Teleia, Hera Chera: maiden, wife, and also woman on the other side of marriage, woman separated from her spouse, woman as widow or divorceé.[6]

The Olympians, those most human of gods, represent a late stage in the evolution of classical Greek religion. Many local traditions predated the collection of the most important gods and goddesses into a pantheon—a divine bureaucracy located on Mount Olympus. On the whole, Indo-European notions seem to predominate over notions from Old Europe. Thus Hera is not the earth mother or the stiff white lady so much as the airy mother of all, the wife of the king of the gods. The Orphics, a spiritualist group interested in the immortality of the human soul and the mysteries of regeneration after death, identify Hera with the air, breezes, and rains. But the nourishment she gives delights the soul as much as the body or the earth. Perhaps the wind best symbolized the pervasiveness of her divine feminine fertility. Perhaps the Orphics enjoyed intuitions similar to those later parlayed by Christians into a divine Spirit brooding holiness in souls as it would.

Whatever the connections, Hera is the heavenly breath that fertilizes the world. She is also the complete woman, holding together the three main stages of the feminine life cycle. Though her main stance is in the center, as wife of the king of the gods, she is youthful, often exhibiting the beauty of the maiden yet to carry the burdens of marriage and childbearing. Downing, however, most identifies with her later phase, in which she is not so much the old woman (crone) become wise at the price of haggardness as the woman separated from her husband and so returned to independence, solitude, and self-sufficiency.

Classical Greeks lived in a patriarchal culture. Men might like women, even find some women intellectually stimulating, but their stronger orientation was to their fellow men. Adult Greeks were remarkably religious, attuned to otherworldly dimensions of virtually all significant experiences.[7] Their regard of their deities ranged from literal worship of Zeus, Hera, the other Olympians, and local divinities to cultured suspicion that such divinities were largely symbolic. The vast majority of adults, though, took the traditional divinities seriously.

Hera and the other goddesses of fertility attracted the prayers of women and men seeking offspring. Hera was the special patroness of marriage, the archetypal wife. Even though some of the Olympian myths portrayed her as bad-tempered or much tried by the unfaithful Zeus, she retained a considerable dignity. As queen of heaven, mother, and spouse, she required respect. Often she stood for the sanctity of the marital bond, in contrast to the irregularity of Zeus, and so she could appear suspicious of erotic attractions, thinking them threats to fidelity.

The genius of complicated mythologies like that of classical Greece is their willingness to sustain opposing symbolisms. On the one hand, the Olympians frolic and commit adultery with such license that Plato censured their mythology as likely to corrupt the morals of students. On the other hand, a Hera emerges to champion marital fidelity. The lesson is that human beings are both faithful and unfaithful. Even if they need master stories to call them to fidelity, the tales from which they take their orientation in life have to provide for their weaknesses. What does this tell us about realistic views of human nature?

First, it tells us that realistic views of human nature cannot be rigid, dogmatic, or legalistic. They have to provide for human fragility, complexity, and ambiguity. Psychologically, people require assurances of forgiveness and invitations to make new starts. These are compatible with injunctions to high moral standards, though precisely how is hard to clarify. Socially, groups need to encourage fidelity to moral obligations without becoming puritanical, judgmental, and unbending. They need to distinguish between major ruptures of trust and ruptures that are minor, to be expected. The Olympian mythology portrays Zeus as more lustful and unfaithful than Hera. In reaction, Hera is jealous and suspicious. Are these stereotypes rooted in universal experience, or are they peculiar to the orientational stories of the Greeks? Ought women to consider infidelity a major or a minor offense? Perhaps virtue lies between the self-indulgence of Zeus and the suspicion of erotic attraction that Zeus caused in Hera. Perhaps the difficult trick is to hate the destructiveness of adultery without closing the door to forgiveness and renewal.

Second, the repertoire of mythical images of women should include not only symbols of fertility and death but also symbols of marital experience and women's passage along the life cycle: from free youth to connected, engaged maturity, and then to the independence that death forces all human beings to contemplate. How free female youths could be in classical patriarchies is a good question, but the myths portray lovely girls approaching the flower of their beauty relatively untrammeled. Still, a virginal, independent femininity may not be the ideal condition. Even though goddesses such as Athena remain striking figures, the majority of divine females, both in Greek mythology and that of other lands, have connections with males.

The world over, the mythmakers have to provide for the basic bisexuality of humankind. Procreation and romantic love are too powerful to neglect. In patriarchal cultures it is difficult to make wives equal to husbands. The best that the myths of Hera can do is grant her a queenly dignity. She should be reverenced, not because of her power, which is not equal to that of Zeus, but because of her station, or being. The more highly developed the soul of the human being contemplating her, the more dignity it will accord her. The infidelities of Zeus, and her own reactions of jealousy, anger, and suspicion of erotic love, diminish this dignity. They make her human, and so approachable, but at the price of tarnishing her beauty and pride. Even when Zeus is clearly in the wrong, we may think that Hera must have failed him.

The analogues in the experiences and images of wronged women persist throughout history, down to the present day. Becoming a wife means risking being considered dull, less attractive than single women, inclined to suspicions, jealousies, and self-serving supports of rigorous moral codes—all in order to hang onto one's husband. And if one's husband is unfaithful, even sympathetic people can seem to wonder about his wife's responsibility. Something went wrong with them as a couple, so probably they should share the blame. Wives themselves are the first to think this way. So to be married to a male like Zeus is to be humiliated. The Greek mythologists were wise to offer wronged wives reasons to think Hera could understand their feelings. If their myths eased the prayers of tearful women, they were great benefactors.

Third, what are the therapies available to present-day women who have been wronged? Beyond recourse to the law and the circle of her true friends, where can today's shamed woman go? Not, I think, to Hera or classical Greece. Few present-day women can pray to Hera as a credible representative of transcendent divinity. At best she is likely to be a psychological comfort. Downing's book succeeds as well as one could hope, granted the intrinsic limits of the Greek materials. It is a sophisticated, sympathetic appropriation of the psychological insights of Greek mythology. In my view, however, it will instruct more women than it will heal or comfort deeply.

Why? Because, with apologies to psychology, we cannot be our own sources of comfort, healing, and forgiveness when the question is the radical crack in creation, the horrifying appearance in our own lives of the mystery of original sin, structural iniquity. The forgiveness we beg for being vulnerable to this mystery, as well as to people who wound others and so bring this mystery into their lives, has to come from outside our own psyches. If the healing of our hurts is nothing more than manipulating the images in our minds or the feelings in our hearts, it remains deeply suspect. Perhaps we are only talking to ourselves, whistling in the dark. Perhaps our faith is only a pep talk, and so our healing is not radical.

The great advantage of the religions that have broken through psychology to a truly transcendent divinity is that they can offer healing, salvation, that seems objective. From a holy force outside my unholy self I can receive a new beginning, a radical cleansing, a healing so intimate that afterward I can barely see the scars of my original wounds. The action has shifted to a God independent of my thoughts, feelings, and being. The mythology has expanded so as to become a divine revelation—a story it had not entered the human heart to conceive.

So, fourth, truly theistic, transpsychological feminists are bound to put a stiff challenge to devotees of the Goddess religion. Are not the new witches, however positive, offering a species of self-salvation? Are they not Pelagians, people unaware of the gratuity of any genuine salvation, because unaware how deep healing has to go, how far the human being has to travel to find that for which it has been made? The majority of the new witches do not claim that the Goddess they venerate is the objective creator of the world. The majority speak in psychological terms, treating the Goddess as a rich, many-sided symbol of the potential of the human imagination, affectivity, and intelligence.

Certainly, the gathering of numerous women, in a spirit of sisterhood, to clarify this potential, affirm it, and bring it to actuality can create powerful feelings of renewal and bonding. Certainly, one should not prefix "merely" to "psychological," as though what is psychological is bound to be trivial or tame in its emotional impact. Still, for a woman of Christian upbringing nothing in the Goddess religion approaches the depth and power of the cross of Christ.

Despite the problems that the history of Christian sexism or the maleness of the Christian savior can raise, I find overwhelmingly more significant the claim of Christian faith (and mythology, in the sense of more-than-historical story) that really, objectively, in space and time, for all people, the death and resurrection of Christ reset the human condition. What were dead ends came back to life, opened up. What were dashed hopes were reassembled. People who had felt useless, humiliated, stripped of dignity received a champion. Like them in all things except sin, well versed in all the variants of human suffering, he brought divinity to bear on their worries and pains, transforming them completely. The love that took him through the cross to the resurrection was the love that had created the world. The experiences of the efficacy of that love were the moving presence of his Spirit. If one abided in that Spirit, one could feel one's woefulness wash away. For the Spirit whispered that God knows, personally, what it is like to be betrayed, humiliated, flayed, crucified. God knows the depths of despair, where everything seems dark and empty.

And, knowing all this, God overcomes it. Objectively, as well as psychologically, there is new creativity, life beyond apparent barrenness and death. In my impression, the new religion of the Goddess does not speak in accents as radical as these. It does not claim ontological changes in the human condition. It cannot go much beyond the moving example of Hera. It does not speak in any literal way of union with a deathless divinity who has promised to wipe away every tear from our eyes. So, if I am correct, the neopagan religions now offered to women need a great deal of work. The Goddess has to become the God/ess who made us from nothingness and loves us eternally. Otherwise, we remain unsaved, undivinized.

ARTEMIS

In her beautifully illustrated work on myths of the Goddess, Manuela Dunn Mascetti uses Artemis as a good example of the virginal woman—the woman enjoying independence, single-mindedness, and freedom from erotic attachments or divisions of her creative energy. The following is Mascetti's digest of the Greek mythology of Artemis:

Artemis was the daughter of Zeus, the chief God of the Greek pantheon, and of Leto. When Hera, the wife of Zeus, discovered the amorous intrigue she became so jealous and enraged that she sent the serpent Python to pursue pregnant Leto and decreed that she should not be delivered in any place where the sun shone. Leto came at last to Ortygia, where she bore Artemis painlessly. As soon as little Artemis was born she helped her mother across narrow straits and there she delivered her of Apollo, after nine days of labor. One day, while she was still a small child, her father Zeus asked her what presents she would like. Artemis answered at once: "Pray, give me eternal virginity; as many names as my brother Apollo; a bow and arrows like his; the office of bringing light; a saffron tunic with a red hem reaching to my knees; and many nymphs from the ocean as my maids of honor." Zeus granted all this and made her guardian of the roads and harbors of thirty cities. Artemis was already patron of childbirth as her mother Leto carried her and bore her with no pain. She asked the Cyclops to build for her a silver bow and some arrows, in return for which they would eat the first prey she brought down. Artemis required the same perfect chastity from her companions as she practiced herself. On one occasion Actaeon stood leaning against a rock to watch Artemis bathing in a stream. Lest he should afterwards dare boast to his companions that she had displayed herself naked in his presence, she changed him into a stag and commanded her own pack of hounds to tear him to pieces.[8]

Artemis, then, is a formidable female. Feminists looking for symbols of independence and strength are bound to find her attractive. She reminds both women and men that femininity has virtues and rights apart from its correlation with masculinity. And by appearing in vigorous pursuits such as hunting, she escapes any potential cloying in a "virginal" life thought of as sequestered from male energy or physical force. She is not a soft woman. No one, least of all Actaeon, would call her effete.

The fate of Actaeon, however, shows the dangers latent in such feminine singlemindedness. When the mere presence of the masculine offends the feminine psyche, destructiveness is bound to follow. Chastity cannot be understood puritanically. Independence and self-determination require a sense of proportion, even a sense of humor. Perhaps Actaeon was presumptuous. Perhaps he was hoping to boast to his buddies of a sneaky peek. But Artemis could have won a more striking victory by keeping her peace and letting him languish. Voyeurism is not attractive, but neither is it satisfying. Real men want more honest interactions. When they declare the honorable intentions necessary for honest interactions, women can decide what sort of chastity is appropriate.

Several further lines of inquiry lie open, however. Inasmuch as voyeurism may be the entryway to unwanted advances or even rape, Artemis is wise to make her "no" definitive. Inasmuch as pleasing men physically can become a great burden for women, privacy, even modesty, can counteract a source of much pain. Nowadays, if not throughout most periods of history, women can become obsessed with how they look—how men, in particular, regard them. From this obsession can come eating disorders, preoccupation with clothes and makeup, great wastes of time and money, and much depression, even suicide.

Henry Jaglom's film *Eating* puts this syndrome into painful focus. Wealthy southern California women gather to celebrate the birthdays of three women, one thirty, one forty, and one fifty. In the course of their gathering, rivers of pain spill out. The majority confess to an obsession with food. (The party has occasioned lavish displays of cakes, rolls, salads, and other foods. The excess of the wealthy is on stunning display.) But food is merely a symbol for the dividedness of the women's psyches. They go to food for comfort when they are depressed, but they fear overeating, gaining weight, feeling unattractive, and becoming more depressed. Indeed, most of them hate their bodies and are deeply unhappy with their selves. Their affluence allows them to become horribly narcissistic, but even when viewers are disgusted by the women's self-centeredness, their pain is too intense to ignore. Indeed, the astute viewer realizes that even poor women, women indentured to children and boring jobs, are not free of worries about how they look, what they can and cannot eat, whether their bodies have not betrayed them, whether they have any real worth. Inasmuch as Artemis suggests freedom from doubts and disorders such as these, she comes as a breath of fresh air.

Once again I find myself searching for a point of balance. If Artemis is too cold and destructive, Aphrodite, the beautiful goddess of sexual desire, is too hot, manipulative, and self-satisfied. Similarly, if the women in Eating are pitiable, the men hinted in the background (the fathers and husbands who appear in the vignettes about the women's feeling fat, unattractive, neglected, and unloved) are maddening. Through selfishness or cloddishness, they have failed their daughters and wives miserably. So the responsibility for women's excessive need to feel good about themselves has to be laid at the door of both sexes. Until being sexually attractive to men is dethroned as women's reason to feel good, if not women's very reason to be, we shall have no health about food or the female body. Naturally, mature men want more from women, whether their daughters or their wives, than a svelte figure. Most men, though, seem to send women a message at best mixed. Is there any hope for improving this situation?

Three helps come to mind. The first is better education of men, and women, through franker discussion. Men have to realize their role in women's so frequent feelings of self-doubt. Fathers (and mothers) have to encourage a proper quotient of Artemis in the development of their daughters. Husbands have to help their wives keep beauty and food in perspective. When family members eat, exercise, and pray together, discussing their problems and feelings frankly but lightly, they all have a better chance to feel supported, keep perspective, and so gain peace, good health, and faith.

Second, whatever reminds people of the objective sufferings of the human race is a good antidote to narcissistic worries. Remembering the people whose main problem is not having enough to eat can help the affluent keep food in its proper place. When we have the leisure to be preoccupied with clothes, diets, or our attractiveness, we need a better job, hobby, or volunteer cause. We need more contact with people who do not have such leisure, who can seldom be self-indulgent, whose needs are much grosser and so, in many ways, more real than our own.

This relates, third, to having a viable religion. If people are immersed in a tradition that presents self-control, asceticism, and sacrifice as helps toward spiritual growth, the love of God, they have solid alternatives to the self-indulgence broadcast to them by the affluent societies. If they have theologies that assure them that God cares more about their minds and hearts than their wardrobes or weights, they have bases for thinking their way to much better self-images. People unhappy, suffering from substantial disorders, will still require sympathetic professional help. Doctors and psychologists will still provide necessary services. But more ultimate, religious wisdoms will be attacking the underlying problem, the basic cultural malaise.

The women in the film *Eating* are godless, in the sense that "God" only appears on their lips as a desperate prayer for relief from their depression, their self-loathing. They seem utterly ignorant of any profound spiritual tradition, Western or Eastern. Their pain tells them that their current worldview is not working, but they see no alternatives. Mammon has them trapped, and mammon is torturing them. A realistic, balanced, healthy religion could show them the way to joy, that wonderful emotion that breaks out when God is our center and we can laugh at ourselves, body and soul together.

3

Asian Cultures

KALI

We begin our reflections on Asian myths concerned with women by confronting Kali, perhaps the most gruesome of the world's many associations of femininity with death. If the stiff white lady of Old Europe gives one pause, Kail gives one the shivers. Consider, for example, the following description of how Kali sprang from the brow of Durga, the Great Goddess, when the need arose for a fierce champion against evil:

The gods have collectively petitioned the Great Goddess (who previously had promised to assist them whenever they found themselves in difficulty), and she has appeared. She calms the worried throng of gods and goes forth to battle the demon hosts [who have subdued them]. The first demon heroes sent forth to battle her are Canda and Muna. When they approach Durga with drawn swords and bent bows, she becomes furious, her face becoming dark as ink. Suddenly there springs forth from her brow the terrible goddess Kali, armed with a sword and noose. She is adorned with a garland of human heads, wears a tiger's skin, and waves a staff with a skull handle. She is gaunt, with sunken, reddish eyes, gaping mouth, lolling tongue and emaciated flesh. She fills the four quarters with her terrifying roar and leaps eagerly into the fray. She flings demons into her mouth and crushes them in her jaws. She wades through the demon hosts, decapitating and crushing all who stand before her. Laughing and howling loudly, she approaches Canda and Munda, grasps them by the hair, and in one furious instant decapitates them both with her mightly sword. Returning to Durga with the two heads, she laughs jokingly and presents them to the Goddess as a gift.[1]

In India the Great Goddess could take various forms. Even though different goddesses appeared to express her functions as wife, mother, patroness of the arts, source of all living things, womb of death, and avenger of the good against their evil foes, popular religion found no difficulty tolerating them all. Instinctively, traditional Hindus knew that all manifestations of the Goddess were united in a great cosmic force.

Running the universe were the twin powers of masculinity and femininity, passivity (a male ideal) and activity, the lingam (phallus) and the yoni (vulva). Even though this dualism meant that masculinity and femininity gathered to themselves different attributes, both sides of the cosmic sexual dimorphism were involved in a full range of emotions, images, and functions. Thus there was a feminine wrath as well as a more expectable feminine gentleness. There was a feminine concern with death as well as a feminine concern with life. So Kali was not the only goddess, and she did not have to carry the full burden of sacral femininity. She sprang from the brow of Durga (a goddess more broadly gauged, closer to the Mahadevi, or Great Goddess) when the need arose to punish terrible wickedness with even more terrible vengeance.

We should underscore, first, that though Kali enjoys her mission of vengeance, she is a force for good. To punish wickedness is a good deed. It sets the cosmos straight. It frees the innocent from the jails of the evil. Indian cosmology tolerated demons, but it was anxious to limit their power. On the symbolic level, there is no mystery of iniquity in Hinduism. There are only powerful forces opposing the good. Fortunately, more powerful forces are at work opposing the evil, both bad human beings and wicked demons. When pushed to explain the origins of these forces in human experience, more philosophical Hindus could only say, "ignorance." This is parallel to the Western tendency to picture evil as the work of Satan but explain it as due to "sin." Neither symbolism nor explanation does the job fully. Each affirms the containment of evil, without proving it. The very intensity of the symbolism associated with Kali testifies to the strength of the Hindu desire to affirm that evil gets its cosmic comeuppance. So, despite her horrible appearance, Kali fights on the side of the angels, for the psychic health of humankind.

Second, the regalia of Kali, which became stylized in Hindu art, are symbols of death. In other iconography, she laps blood. The tiger's skin makes her seem primitive, a force of nature. She mauls and kills as naturally, as swiftly and gracefully, as a tigress. Her ascetic appearance sometimes associated her with Shiva, the male god of destructiveness and asceticism. She represents in a feminine mode all the battles that must be waged against evil, both physical and spiritual. If the good soldier is the main agent of battle against physical evil, the ascetic is the main agent in the battle against spiritual evil. By warring against the ignorant, sinful flesh, the ascetic gains the power of holiness. Holiness is a power, all the more so in cultures where its primordial associations with nature remain strong. The remarkable being of nature—the super-reality of oceans and heavens, storms and blistering droughts, animal procreation and death—requires the human beings immersed in it to bow low in wonder and petition. Kali trades on these deep emotions. She is the goddess of death, one of the most powerful forces in both nature and the psyche.

The mouth of Kali is the great organ of death. Her sword is significant, but her maw is more impressive. In some Hindu mythologies it becomes the symbol of time. Everything created moves toward her to be devoured. Here she is laying about like a great warrior, but in other scenarios she waits sinisterly, sure that everything will finally come to her. These scenarios suggest that even though Kali is a goddess working on the side of goodness, the death with which she is so closely associated afflicts the innocent as well as the guilty.

The forces of death and destruction are not so immaculate, so sanitized, that they hit all their targets with no collateral damage. Built into the structures of the cosmos is a scatter-shot necessity that all living things come to an end. So even her devotees would approach Kali cautiously, as the devotees of Shiva would approach him cautiously. Where other goddesses smiled like welcoming mothers, the motherhood of Kali was the entranceway to death. Curiously, as noted, this entranceway is usually her mouth. She is not a goddess whose womb connotes the tomb of burial. We have to associate her with eating, devouring, consuming—all the oral overtones of the march of time, all the consumption of natural resources and human potential.

Last, perhaps it is profitable to muse about Kali's dreadful appearance. She shows that divine femininity can move beyond any concern for beauty, comeliness, or being attractive. Artemis remained free of great concern for how men regarded her, because she had no desire to become attached to a man. Kali seems to exult in her dreadful appearance. Certainly, one can find a macabre beauty in her gaunt, ashen appearance. She is not obese or grotesque. But her hair is matted, her eyes are red, her bearing is wild. She laughs on the edge of madness, as though driven beyond control by the evil with which she has to deal. She is dangerous, the antithesis of the safe female, the soft welcoming bosom. It might be salutary for women like those portrayed in the film *Eating* to study the iconography of Kali and discuss what it makes them think about their appearance—how Kali relativizes all soft, safe criteria for beauty.

I find the symbolism of Kali more useful than disturbing. It reminds me that both sexes have to fight against evil and that women have a rage to contribute to this fight. It also says that women's rage, like that of men, can become unbridled, threatening to destroy the good as well as the evil. And so it puts femininity on a relatively equal footing with masculinity. Neither sort of primitive sexuality, creativity, or energy is fully good or fully evil. Both have to be directed, purified, understood, mastered, redeemed.

Futhermore, Kali is a wonderful antidote to the too-soft, cloy-ing versions of femininity that we find in many discussion groups and in some Goddess symbolism. Kali is close to nature, and nature is not all teddy bears and pink flowers. Women do well to ponder their rages, sources of destructiveness, and associa-tions with death. They do well to think about the connections between bringing forth children and anointing the bodies of the dead. Traditionally, women have stood at the terminals of hu-man existence, been both the beginning and the end. Thus the Virgin Mary brings forth the Christ child, and the female disci-ples head for Jesus' tomb to anoint his body for burial.

What kind of warfare ought women to wage nowadays? What associations with birth and death are the healthiest? Should women have equal opportunity to fly planes in combat, assault dug-in enemy positions with mortars and rifles? Should women be on display as boxers, wrestlers, participants in "contact" sports? Thinking about Kali suggests that these questions have no easy answers. The angry, warring female shakes up our stereo-types, forcing us to reconsider female potential, for both good and evil.

On balance, however, I think that women are wise to con-tinue to associate themselves with the life-giving, life-protecting imagery of the motherly goddesses and the nurturing forces of their culture, because men have yet to give these forces equal weight. Were men more reluctant warriors, antagonists, and reservoirs of rage, women might be free to express their emotions as they wished. At the moment, raging women further tip the balance of our American culture against peacemaking and the inner quiet necessary to hear God.

Certainly, I applaud women's resistance to evil, their marshal-ing energy to oppose rape, domestic violence, and all other forms of abuse against women, children, the poor, the weak, and the sickly. Certainly, I note with favor women's leadership among the advocates for the homeless, the handicapped, and those trying to make do on welfare or medicare or frozen pensions. Women do well to form caucuses to fight sexism in the churches, in business offices, and in the advertising industry. And all of this requires a hatred of physical abuse and cultural injustice. All of it legitimates a righteous anger, a holy rage.

But Kali cannot be all. Even the mothers fighting so hard against drunk drivers, the women working for gun control, and the female soldiers in the lobbies for more attention to AIDS do best when they alternate the grim visage of holy rage with the fair side of faith that we all lie in God's keeping, that one day all will be well. It is hard to picture a conversation between Kali and Julian of Norwich, who was convinced that in God all manner of thing is already well, but that is the picture now drawing me. On the razor's edge of sanctity, far from where I now stand, the two symbolisms seem complementary.

THE PRAJNAPARAMITA

The various great religious cultures have told women that they represent the fertility of the earth, the frightening power of death, the enticing warmth of the wife, and the cool mystery of the virgin. The myths that women have heard as little children, contemplated as adults, and often treasured in old age have offered deep spiritual nourishment. Feminine human nature has appeared to be as rich as masculine. To be a woman has offered a great range of meaningful possibilities, many of them subtle and beguiling. Indeed, precisely the subtlety of feminine intelligence seems to account for the persistent association of mythical women with wisdom. The Great Goddess is a more frequent symbol of the understanding that has gone beyond worldly partiality, that reposes in the heaven or ultimacy where things are whole, than are the corresponding male symbols of understanding. In cultures dominated by male doubts about female nature, the complexity, variety, delicacy, grace, and general richness of feminine ways seem to have made ties between wisdom and a feminine visage, voice, and assurance that all is well arise naturally, spontaneously, like an obvious gift of nature.

So, for example, it requires little stretching of the imagination to picture the Buddhist symbol of wisdom, the Lady Prajnaparamita, reconciling the rage of Kali with the peaceful confidence of Julian of Norwich. For the Prajnaparamita, the same female countenance could token both the lifegiver and the lifetaker, both the mother and the stiff white lady. Why? Because the Prajnaparamita dwells beyond all worldly dualisms. She speaks from nirvana, the far side of reality, the source of all unity, stability, secure and holy meaning. The Mahayana Buddhist schools that most liked to contemplate the Prajnaparamita thought that nirvana had to exist within, at the foundations of samsara, the realm of change, suffering, and contingency. Nirvana is the realm we enter by blowing out the flame of desire. Nirvana is the state of the candle (ourselves) when the flame is gone. Nirvana is peace, unconcern, compassion. Nirvana is like the stillness of the Christian hesychasts: the state of dispassion, the condition in which one can give full attention to ultimacy and live with a glorious grace.

The beginning and concluding verses of the Heart Sutra, a brief but brilliant specimen of the Prajnaparamita literature, exemplify the place of Lady Wisdom in Mahayana Buddhist meditative philosophy: "Homage to the Perfection of Wisdom, the Lovely, the Holy! . . . Therefore one should know the prajnaparamita as the great spell, the spell of great knowledge, the utmost spell, the unequalled spell, allayer of all suffering, in truth—for what could go wrong? By the prajnaparamita has this spell been delivered. It runs like this: Gone, gone, gone beyond, gone altogether beyond, O what an awakening, all-hail—This completes the Heart of perfect wisdom."[2]

Edward Conze, the translator of these verses, makes it clear that the invocation with which the sutra begins addresses a feminine deity.

The word *Bhagavati*, which I have translated as Lovely, can also be translated as "Lady." *Arya* is not only "holy," but also "noble," and is an attribute of the Buddhas and of those of their disciples who have definitely turned away from this world to the world of the spirit. . . . It is difficult to say about this invocation much that is of use to the general reader. Its repetition should help us to raise our minds in reverence to the perfection of wisdom, as the mother of the Buddhas, as our guide through the world, and as the embodiment of perfect purity. Devotion may be strengthened by the contemplation of images, and by recalling the thirty-two epithets of wisdom.[3]

The contemplation of images reminds us that in the invocation we are dealing with a mandala (sacred image). When we study the concluding verses of the Heart Sutra, it will be plain that we are also dealing with a mantra (sacred sound). The Prajnaparamita is a feast for both the eye and the ear. Interiorly, it is what Buddhist meditators of philosophical bent have long loved to gaze upon and chant. There is something almost sensual or erotic in this orientation. Conze stresses the purity of Lady Wisdom, which connotes a chasteness of intellect. But the contemplative imagination seems to bore into this noble goddess, while the contemplative sense of speech and hearing delights in chanting her attributes. She presents a softness and beauty that is welcoming, almost seductive. She is gentle and rounded, nourishing and fertile. So she is a prospective lover, suggesting all spiritual delights. To attain union with the Wisdom that has gone beyond all this-worldly desire or partiality is to gain a nuptial bliss.

Why does ultimate Buddhist wisdom carry the smile, the allure, of a gracious female? Perhaps because Gautama's experience of enlightenment, from which Buddhism derives, took him into a realm of beauty and peace. It removed him from the strife of desire, the need constantly to fight his wayward flesh and mind. It removed the soul-deep fear that observing death, disease, and aging had insinuated. Enlightenment liberated the Buddha. The knowledge that flooded his soul took him apart from the world, into the gist of nirvana.

Like a beautiful hostess, Lady Wisdom stands at the entry to nirvana. She welcomes those who have cast aside ignorance, making them feel at home. So all seekers after wisdom pay homage to her. In bowing low to her beauty, they acknowledge that their quest is for a positive perfection. They are not fleeing the world only because they hate corruption and death, evil and stupidity. They are drawn by intimations of a light, a peace, a compassion for which they feel made. When they shed the self-centeredness and illusion of karmic bondage, they will fly to the highest heavens of contentment. That is the positive connotation of the far-sidedness of Lady Wisdom. She stands beyond the streams of suffering, like the reward the good warrior or navigator deserves.

Lady Wisdom is also the mother of all Buddhas. In Buddhist cosmology, the universe, all reality, issues forth from the womb of knowledge. A buddha is a knowledge being, one who has become flooded with light. For much Mahayana philosophy, this light is intrinsic to being. To gain Buddhahood is simply to realize what one has always been and to realize what all other beings are, when one perceives them wisely. Reality, suchness, is perfect in its own right. The problem and puzzle is why we are ignorant of such perfection.

The answer lies in our desire, though why we have this desire is never made fully clear. As long as we want things, are striving and full of appetite, we shall never see correctly, never be correctly. Peace will elude us. All our judgments and choices will mix darkness and light, mix folly with any wisdom we manage to gain. So the Buddhists created an attractive persona for the wisdom that those serious about enlightenment would contemplate. They offered the Lady Prajnaparamita: beautiful, gracious, welcoming, pure—everything the noble, Aryan spirit could desire without binding itself further to karmic suffering.

The main teaching of the Heart Sutra is that all things are empty. Nothing that human beings experience is independent, an "own-being," something worth desiring. This includes the human composite itself. There is no stable self. There is no permanent, full identity to which to cling. Wisdom involves freeing oneself from the delusion of a permanent, stable selfhood. It entails floating free of attachments, including the most pernicious attachment: to one's own "I." At the beginning of this demanding process stands the gracious Lady Wisdom, welcoming the struggler and suggesting that the struggle is well worthwhile. At the end of the sutra and the process stands the Goddess more fully revealed. She is the great spell, the magical power, of enlightenment.

The sutra plays on the word for "gone," to drum home the beyondness, the far-sidedness—what the Westerner would call the transcendence—of Lady Wisdom and nirvana. The Sanskrit *gate gate paragate parasamgate* ("gone, gone, gone beyond, gone altogether beyond") is the heart of the mantra, the sacred sounding, with which the sutra concludes. The assumption was that the earnest disciple would chant these words repeatedly, almost hypnotically, to enter the state of spirit necessary to appreciate the beauty of going beyond—leaving worldly ideas and detachments, dwelling in intention in nirvana, wisdom, fulfillment. This is the spell, the mantra, the chanting, the intentional state of soul that allays all suffering. When in its grasp, which is the open-armed embrace of the Prajnaparamita, what could go wrong? One has been welcomed to the bosom of ultimate reality. All the sources of suffering have fallen away and been left far behind.

The message, then, is that reality itself is perfect, and we human beings can enter into this perfection. Reality itself is not pain, suffering, evil, or illusion. If we quit our fascination with the world and ourselves, if we exit from the grasp of the senses and our gross feelings, we can realize the substance of human potential: the flooding of the spirit with light, freedom, and beauty. The awakening that comes in this exodus from sensuality and worldliness is the Great Awakening that religious seekers have always pursued. It is what made Gautama the Buddha, what was visited upon all the other buddhas and bodhisattvas (saints who will become buddhas). It is ineffable, requiring exclamations to suggest the little that poetic speech can. It is blissful, as one would expect anything perfect to be. Above all, it is the essence of wisdom. To know reality as it truly is, is to be filled with inexpressible joy.

This text needs little further commentary to suggest the comforts it might offer women. Deep in the Buddhist mythology of enlightenment lies a warm, resounding affirmation of essential femininity. Beyond strife, in the embrace of ultimacy, we find the best of mothers, the one we have been seeking since being forced from the womb. We also find the best of lovers, the most beautiful of muses, the gentlest and so most effective of teachers. The Wisdom that has gone beyond is subtle, dextrous, intuitive. It deals in secrets that ordinary logic, worldly reasoning, cannot unlock. It is simple and alluring. Only those willing to purify themselves, like knights seeking to be worthy of their ladies fair, will gain access to it. It need not threaten, come in the guise of blood-dripping death. It stands apart from, beyond, all need to combat evil, overcome death, make amends for injustices and sufferings. Simply to be with it, enjoy its presence, delight in its beauty is the redemption of one's constitutive hopes. It is, in Western parlance, heaven: the beatifying vision and love of God.

Contrary to Western imagery, however, it is feminine. If given a face, Buddhist heavenly bliss appears as a Madonna, a lover, a sisterly charmer. What Beatrice was to Dante—lover, friend, teacher, muse—the Prajnaparamita is to the Buddhist meditator of philosophical bent. What Beatrice told Western women about their best services to men, or any people wanting to envision the divine comedy of human potential, the Prajnaparamita has told Eastern women. Nowadays, as our religious culture becomes global, she beckons as a great resource for Western women as well. At the depths of the contemplative life, she gives the ways of women a resounding affirmation. If we trust to our best instincts about wisdom and love, we may enter upon a beauty we now barely can hope will be the substance of our fulfillment.

AMATERASU

The Japanese sun goddess, Amaterasu, tells us interesting things about Japanese femininity. In the mythical strata of the

Japanese psyche, the queen of heaven fought against her brother, the rude wind god, Susanoo. Let us begin with a text from the *Nihongi*, one of two chronicles of early, indigenous traditions on which Shinto, the native Japanese religion, depends.

> After this Susa-no-o no Mikoto's behavior was exceedingly rude. In what way? Amaterasu (the Heaven-Shining-Deity) had made august rice fields of Heavenly narrow rice fields and Heavenly long rice fields. Then Susa-no-o, when the seed was sown in spring, broke down the divisions between the plots of rice, and in autumn let loose the Heavenly piebald colts, and made them lie down in the midst of the rice fields. Again, when he saw that Amaterasu was in her sacred weaving hall, engaged in weaving garments of the Gods, he flayed a piebald colt of Heaven, and breaking a hole in the roof-tiles of the hall, flung it in. Then Amaterasu started with alarm, and wounded herself with the shuttle. Indignant of this, she straightway entered the Rock-cave of Heaven, and having fastened the Rock-door, dwelt there in seclusion. Thereafter constant darkness prevailed on all sides, and the alternation of night and day was unknown.[4]

Generally in the world religions, the sun is considered a male deity, married to the female earth. Earth is the mother, sun the father. Earth presents a potentially fertile womb, open to the sky. The sky provides fertilizing rain, light, and warmth. From the interaction of the two, the sacred marriage, comes the fertility on which plants, animals, and human beings all depend. It is unusual, then, to find a sun goddess. Amaterasu may not be unique in the annals of goddesses, but she is singular.

From the recorded beginnings of Shinto, which start at the least with the establishment of the national shrine at Ise, very early in the first century A.D., we find the imperial family associated with the sun goddess. She is the primary divine ancestor, and the regalia of the Japanese rulers represent her influence. The Japanese seem to have favored a maternal image in their basic conception of divinity. When Buddhism entered Japan and made a significant impact, about the middle of the sixth century A.D., it paved the way for the great influence of Kannon, a bodhisattva who effectively functioned as a mother goddess. Even today, one finds shrines to Kannon throughout Japan. For example, in the center of Tokyo stands the "baby shrine," a place where those who have petitioned Kannon for children can display their successes: pictures of healthy, usually chubby infants whom the goddess has granted them.

In this selection from the traditional Shinto mythology, we find Amaterasu in conflict with Susanoo, her brother. The stereotypes are fascinating. Clearly, the ancient Japanese sense of the world ran to dichotomies and antagonisms, which it cast in terms of female-male polarities. Amaterasu stands for order, dignity, kindliness, and propriety. Susanoo stands for rebellion, bawdy display, obstreperousness, and adolescent challenge to propriety. He seems to resent the rule of his elder sister. Thus he disrupts the rice fields that she has planted lovingly, like a little girl tending a garden. The piebald colt was an animal unsuited for imperial sacrifice (which demanded pure colors in its victims). For him to place the piebald colts in the rice fields and then flay one and fling it into the weaving room of Amaterasu was to upset the entire order of the ritual sacrifice—the microcosm through which traditional Japan tried to bring the order of heaven down to earth. In other stories, his crude offensiveness even extends to excreting on her imperial throne.

Again and again, Susanoo is the unruly younger brother acting up, rebelling against the gentle order of his older sister, who has taken precedence in the management of humanity's affairs. On one level, the symbolism is of the contest between the stable sun, relatively reliable in its orderly ways, its coursings across the sky, and the unpredictable wind, which comes in storms, can blister the earth in summer, and blows where it will. On another level, the symbolism contrasts the ways of females, ways especially reserved and decorous in traditional Japan, and males, who constantly strive to maintain control, and whose resentment of female rule can be explosive.

The peculiar character of these Shinto myths is their inclination to make the ways of the sun, the ways of traditional females, primary and the ways of the wind, the traditional males, secondary. Perhaps we are dealing with reflections of a childrearing in which elder sisters often stood in for mothers, bossing their younger siblings about. Or perhaps the primary intuition is that order comes from the more peaceable ways of the feminine parts of the human psyche, while problems come from the aggressive, self-assertive male parts. In any case, Amaterasu appears as the aggrieved party, enduring the offensive behavior of her male junior as long as she can, before traipsing off in hurt or wounded dignity. She has done her best to make the land fertile, and she is working at the loom, presumably to provide her people warm clothing. In other words, food and apparel come from her diligence, her maternal care. When Susanoo does not appreciate these benefactions, in fact throws them in her face, violating all sacred propriety as well as all ordinary gratitude, she quits the game. Enough is enough. Having wounded her finger on the shuttle because of his violent irruption into her realm, she withdraws into the rock cave of heaven—the fastness from which the sun had to emerge each morning and to which it returned each night.

As the myth continues, her subjects naturally petition Amaterasu not to deprive them of light and warmth. The earth withers without her ministrations. She waits an expectable time so that the people can appreciate the depth of their need of her and then agrees to resume her services. She has made her point, and Susanoo is properly chastened, in the affections of her subjects if not his own judgment. The paramount need for divine feminine fertility is reestablished in the land. The status of the sun goddess is again clearly supreme. Any temptation to indulge Susanoo, to forget the primacy of order, holy ritual, and the provision of food and clothing, has been dashed. The people realize that they are dealing with a sensitive, though generous, female. She will do everything for them, but she requires a modicum of respect and gratitude. If they hurt her feelings, she will withdraw from the economy of creation, to their great loss. Without a generous feminine fertility, they will languish in darkness and infertility. It behooves them to get their acts of gratitude and veneration back together. It behooves them to reject the temptation to play the wastrel, the rebel, as Susanoo has done. Dramatic and entertaining as naughty Susanoo can be, it is disastrous to follow him.

While the myth gives both sexes something to applaud, it gives greater support to the roles and psychology of women. Necessary as the wind, male energy and unruliness, may be, the greater need is for female constancy and fertility. It is fine for creation to require an interaction, even a contest, between femininity and masculinity, but the overall economy of nature, and society, must reckon with the limits that femininity will endure—the point at which it will quit the game and so jeopardize the entire process. Amaterasu is not far from the women dramatized by the playwright Aristophanes. When the Greek men had exceeded the bounds of propriety, insisting on their warlike ways so strongly that they threatened good order and the survival of culture, the women withdrew their sexual services. Before long, the men were reconsidering their warlike ways. In this case, Amaterasu has withdrawn the entire spectrum of female services. By opting out of the cultural cooperative, because she has been asked to endure too much, she makes it plain that femininity is absolutely essential, and so that it has rights to at least a minimal courtesy, a bare-bones acknowledgment of its dignity and generosity.

The patterns in this comic yet serious myth are all too familiar. By and large, little girls are socialized to niceness, order, pretty and dignified things, ceremonies, and etiquette. Boys chafe at the imposition of such a female order, and necessarily so. To be hunters and warriors, explorers of the realms outside the peaceable hearth, they need a fierce energy, self-reliance, and iconoclasm. But they have to recognize the limits of their violations of what females require. They have to pay some homage to the generosity of females, who assume the major share of the responsibility for bringing life forth and keeping it going. If they play too roughly, they will lose the cooperation of girls and so the fertile spark between the sexes. The play of children of course anticipates and mirrors the interactions of adults. The myth is warning Japanese men not to press Japanese women too far. It is reminding all the Japanese people that they can lose the light and warmth of what should be the sunshine in their lives.

Often women suffer the depredations of men too long. Often they are too nice because they fear conflict too much and because the hurt to their feelings is too painful. On the whole, they do too much for men, and they require too little. Certainly, the syndrome of the princess, who expects to be waited on hand and foot, or of the touchy female (Hera pushed to an extreme) warns us not to canonize feminine behavior or psychology. Both sexes are responsible for the pathologies of culture, including the dysfunctions in their specifically heterosexual interactions. Still, granted this caveat, the prevailing pattern tends to be for men to aggress, overstep the bonds of fair play, ask too much of women, and for women, out of timidity, to refuse to fight back, speak up for themselves, and so defend objective justice. The majority of women who finally throw their misbehaving husbands out confess that they waited far too long. The high percentage of abused women who cannot—will not—admit what their husbands are doing to them and quit the destructive game tells us that we have to support the female psyche in its efforts to learn how to fight back, at least to the extent of defending itself against deadly violence.

Certainly, we may hope that women will learn to fight well without succumbing to male patterns of violence and excess. Certainly, we may continue to love feminine gentleness and dignity. But we have to learn something from Amaterasu. Even in her nonviolent, perhaps overly hurt and sulking mode of retreat, she does the essential thing. She forces Susanoo, and all tempted to indulge his offensive ways, to realize that without her great contributions the social order breaks down. Elementally, she is necessary for food and clothing, to say nothing of refinement, good order, taste, beauty, playfulness, and a dozen other ministrations of Lady Wisdom. Elementally, she has to drive home the point that there are strict limits to the abuse she will endure. When women take this lesson to heart, they are not indulging themselves. Far from it. They are standing up for both their own mental health and the objective needs of their entire society. Indeed, unless they do stand up in this way, they become conspirators with abusive males in the great damage done to the entire race, especially the children, by male abuse of female niceness.

RADHA

In the Hindu pantheon, Krishna is the most beloved deity. An *avatar*, or manifestation of Vishnu, Krishna not only advises the warrior Arjuna in the Bhagavad Gita, perhaps the most acclaimed Hindu scripture, he also functions as the divine lover, romancing the souls of those desiring mystical union, especially the souls of women. Krishna is a mischievous youth, and during young adulthood he is a passionate lover. In both guises, he has won over, even tormented, many traditional Hindu females. However, they have had to share him with Radha, his childhood sweetheart and wife. To share him, many Hindu women have identified themselves with Radha, making her the ideal female lover and spouse. She is beautiful. Krishna steals her heart. She remains faithful to him, even when he is unfaithful to her. In all ways she is the paradigmatic female, willing and able to give herself wholeheartedly to the male, human or divine, who has brought her to herself as a female.

One indication of the popular mythical persona of Radha comes from the following description of how she appears in the vernacular poetry of Braj, an area of the Uttar Pradesh where she is the premier deity. The collection of poems known as the *Sur Sagar* contains many verbal portraits of Radha, some of which have been further realized in miniature paintings. The following portion of an analysis of these verbal portraits suggests the sensuality that Radha, the most faithful of wives, could offer to Krishna (and to the Hindu women modeling themselves upon her):

> A poem that seems to proceed as a straightforward description of Radha's very unstraightforward beauty—the poet emphasizes her snake-like motions, the curvature of her eyebrows, her sidelong glances—turns out in the last line to be not only the poet's description but one offered by Krishna himself. Other times Krishna's vision, as he gazes at Radha, becomes hopelessly complicated: he is unable to believe his senses and wonders if it is all hallucination. Rarely does *Sur* show us Radha and Krishna while they are actually making love. Again it is a question of perspective. They must be seen by some other figure in their world; hence we observe the moment when they emerge from their love nest (or Radha does so alone, Krishna having gone off while she slept). Like the *gopis* [cow-tending girls madly in love with Krishna] who witnessed such a sight, we look beyond their (or her) disheveled state and imagine the battle of love that caused it. Or if the poet takes us to the battleground itself, he is apt to supply us with other perspectives from which to observe what we see, by turning the scuffles of Radha and Krishna into a match between the Love-god himself and his mate or comparing their encounter with the epic stand-off between Arjuna and Karna, a battle [in the *Mahabharata*, the great Hindu epic poem] over which, ironically, Krishna himself presided in quite another guise.[5]

This indirect perspective of the poet Sur suggests the mythical character of his materials. He is not handing over local gossip. He is not writing merely human poetry, drawn from the ordinary strata of the human imagination. He is handing over sacred imagery, tales long believed to tell their hearers something essential about the nature of divinity. Krishna and Radha remain sacral figures, larger than life, even when they are wrestling like young lovers in heat. To confront them head-on, as though one could capture them in a photograph, would be to denature their reality. They have to slide into the psyche indirectly, always be captured through a filtered lens. The hearer has to contribute more than half the portrait because the studio is the sacred portion of the hearer's psyche.

Second, we note the curvature of Radha. She is the ideal Indian woman, rounded in every way. Not for traditional India the stick-line feminine beauty of our current Western fashion magazines. In traditional Indian sculpture the females have hourglass figures, full breasts and hips. They have large eyes and heavy brows made for dramatic glances. When we find them in dancers' poses, they are sinuous, slinking, more likely to weave up and down than perform athletic high kicks. Krishna is bedazzled by this sinuous beauty. The warrior part of him, schooled to military directness, can get no hold on it. It seizes his fancy so completely that he fears for his sanity. Can all this entrancing beauty be real?

Third, the references to the physical love-play between Krishna and Radha remind us that they have stood in the Hindu imagination as marital lovers. Their marriage has been considered passionate, highly erotic. As a symbol for the union between the religious soul and its deity, the union of Radha and Krishna has stood at the center of an immense devotional energy known as bhakti. For the common people, especially the women of the lower classes, passionate, erotic love of the godhead has often been the prime consolation for a difficult life. Especially devout women could send the deepest parts of themselves outside the shabby circumstances of their actual lives, imagining a constant series of trysts with Krishna. The popular artistic inducements to this emotional journeying might sometimes become trashy, on the order of our contemporary midday soap operas, but the divinity of the lover kept it from becoming pornographic. The same with the vernacular poetry. The descriptions seldom come from inside the lovers' bower. The disheveled, abstracted appearance of Radha speaks the delightful volumes.

For our purposes, it is instructive that Radha is not an Aphrodite, a wanton goddess of love. Her sensuality need not operate on its own, apart from marital fidelity. She is not a free-floating female sexuality, enticing men away from their responsibilities, fighting against good social order. Rather, Radha would beguile Krishna into fidelity, offering him at home physical love so intense that he would have no inclination to seek it elsewhere. The descriptions of the early infatuation that brings these two divinities together are highly charged. Krishna and Radha see all that they want in one another. Radha is more faithful to this initial passion than Krishna, but they have a sizable period of marital bliss, before he goes off on military adventures. His absence causes Radha great pain, and she has to suffer assaults on her character because Krishna seems to doubt that any woman could be as faithful as she. But throughout, she remains nearly obsessed with him, and her obsession enters into the profile of the ideal Hindu wife. She is not only faithful and dutiful, she is these things because of her ardent love. She burns only for Krishna, and she burns brightly. She is a good match for his own supernatural ardor, his own hyperbolic sensuality. And so she stimulates the portions of the female psyche where it is delicious to think of an ongoing passion of great intensity. She legitimates female eros by combining it with complete fidelity. Indeed, it is her erotic intensity that keeps her pure regarding all outsiders. They hold no attraction for her, because all her fire flames toward Krishna.

Rarely do religious myths deal so frankly or positively with eros, either female or male. Some mystical literature from the West, glossing the biblical Song of Songs, gets rather heated, but the immediate move is usually allegorical. The mythology of Radha stays closer to physical longings and fulfillments. It deals in love, not lust, but its love is lusty, and proud to be. Radha wants the earth to move. Krishna wants to penetrate the great wonder of his hallucination. The only proper climax to their love is mutually orgasmic. Even when one has to smile at the excesses and improbabilities in the mundane bases of the descriptions, the smile carries more pleasure than cynicism.

It is good for women to come upon reasons to believe that romance is compatible with marital realities and the realities of faith. It is good for them to think that marital relations carry the ardor of God. Making a living and raising children can take a great toll on romance. Radha legitimates the feeling that it should not be so—might not be so, if one did a little planning, provided a little provocation. Obviously, both sexes have to be willing and cooperative, but Radha takes as much initiative as Krishna. She wants their wrestling as much as he, and she is willing to let him know this. So I find myself liking this Hindu goddess and thinking the mythology surrounding her refreshing.

Radha is more than the fertile or forbidding female, more than the seductress unconcerned about the consequences of her liaisons. She is the passionate lover committed heart and soul. Her fidelity is the result of her complete gift of herself, her full gamble that her physical passion will find both consummation and complementarity. Because this is a dangerous gamble, making her highly vulnerable, she shows us a remarkable courage.

Can we still believe in an all-consuming passion? Will time, our selves, or our men allow it? Revealing questions. Radha is a great challenge to feminists, men as well as women. In the stories of her love for Krishna, both the pleasures and the pains of ardor between the sexes become cautionary. Yet, one senses that she would not have it otherwise. Better to have been hurt, badly, than never to have experienced full passion. Better to have glimpsed why divinity has to be a fiery love than to have contented oneself with dutiful pieties.

THE MOON

The association made in medieval China in the thirteenth century A.D. between women and the moon alerts us to another regular facet of feminine mythology in traditional Asia. The following description from Jacques Gernet's fascinating study of daily life in China on the eve of the Mongol invasion is a good introduction to an association taken for granted throughout much of the traditional, mythical world:

> The mid-autumn festival, on the 15th of the 8th moon, was the festival of the moon and of women. In the moon, devoured each month by a black toad, there was a rabbit who pounded an elixir of long life at the foot of an acacia tree, the leaves and bark of which were used in the preparation of the drug. Another legend had it that it was not a rabbit, but a three-legged toad that inhabited the moon; according to yet another, there was a palace there where the queen of the moon and her attendants lived, all of an extraordinary beauty. On the evening of the 15th of the 8th month [the full moon of September], the moon is at its most brilliant. "Moon cakes" were made, and fruit with pips was eaten symbolic of having many children. Rich people went up on to the upper storeys of their pavilions and summer-houses to admire the moonlight and drink rice-wine while listening to solos on the zither. The common people, down to the poorest, bought rice-wine, even if it meant pawning their clothes. The city [Hang-chow] was full of merry-makers that night, and the shops on the Imperial Way stayed open later than usual.[6]

First, we are dealing with a lunar calendar, the periodization of the year that the majority of traditional peoples have favored. It is easier to count the phases of the moon than to determine the passages of the sun.

Second, inasmuch as women's menstrual periodicity has likened them to the moon, traditional time has carried a feminine character. It has gone round and round, rather than straightforward. It has held the promise of remaining familiar, never creating complete novelty, and so checked the terror of radical newness. It would have been terrifying to contemplate a history going straight to nowhere. The mental cosmos that traditional peoples fashioned protected them against chaos—lack of structure to the point of meaninglessness. Women shared in this projection of regularity. They became the sex on which social stability depended. Paradoxically, they could also carry the persona of flightiness, compared to the gravity of the male persona. Still, in their bodies they were dependable. Month by month, they and the moon allowed traditional peoples to chart their course.

Third, this description deals with what people in the West might call the harvest moon. The festival especially dedicated to women occurred when the moon was at its biggest, its most impressive and romantic. The very fullness of the moon seemed to token a universal fertility. The crops were maturing in the field. The year seemed to be completing its time of gestation. Soon it would become fallow, through the darkness and cold of winter. But here it was nearing the climax of its annual pregnancy. Here it was ripe to the point of pride, radiant with the glow of fruitfulness.

Fourth, specialists will have to explain the exact significance of the toad and the rabbit, but a commonsensical interpretation ties them to menstrual experience of both loss and renewed potential. The toad takes away the fertility unused each month, dark like dried blood. The rabbit, randy and prolific, hops in with the cheerful reminder that potential fruitfulness will return soon. To have the rabbit pounding out an elixir of long life is to extend the connotations of fertility to the entirety of the life cycle. People in phase with the moon, glad to go with it round and round, can hope for a long life. The spiritual elixir necessary to live long and well is to integrate one's ways with those of the cosmos.

Something Taoist may be at work here in the background. The Tao (Way of Nature) is the Great Mother, from which issue the 10,000 things of creation. Supreme wisdom and fertility come from going with the grain of the Tao, not working at cross-purposes to nature. So any physical drug is also a symbol of the spiritual attitude needed for survival to a ripe old age. In a ripe old age, a Chinese person could hope to see many grandchildren, perhaps even many greatgrandchildren. They would honor one's longevity, and promise to perform the rites necessary for one's peaceful existence after death. Fertility in traditional China embraced countless generations. Veneration of the ancestors was a way of offering thanks for the preservation of the clan through the centuries, and also a way of petitioning similar good fortune in the future.

Fifth, the queen of the moon and her attendants, extraordinary in their beauty, draw the symbolism of the festival of women back to its human analogues. The delicacy, grace, and lightness of the beautiful Chinese woman refine the beauty of the moon. Fertile she and it are, but not at the price of grossness. The moon always remains cooler than the sun, smaller, more intriguing. The harvest moon, huge and nearly orange, is not fully representative. Delightful and cherished as it may be, it cannot obliterate the many times when the moon is pale and fragile, a mere fingernail of light. Part of the rejoicing in the September festival is for the triumph of female robustness over female fragility. One cannot assume that women will always be robust. Much in their makeup is delicate, vulnerable. A healthy culture honors this, without destroying women's vigor or ignoring their strength. The queen of the moon had to represent upper-class beauties, as well as sturdy peasant mothers. The great span of feminine beauty paralleled the many different phases of the moon.

Last, the celebratory mood of this festival, the determination of all classes to make merry, tells us that it was an unusually happy, blessed time. The message was one of good fortune, reason to have a party. The moon cakes were a special treat, meant to honor the benevolent deity of the sky. The fruit with seeds, symbolic of many children, suggests that in their celebrating, the people hoped for much fruitfulness, especially in their own families. The festival night was made for music, laughter, enjoyment, but nothing raucous or vulgar intrudes. The rice wine merely puts an extra glow on a happy occasion. At the end of the celebration one can imagine much lovemaking, as both the natural climax to a special evening and a final bow to the harvest moon.

Women have to be more pleased than pained by this description of their special festival in medieval China, yet both self-interest and objectivity suggest a critical look. There were many celebrations throughout the traditional Chinese year, so one especially focused on women might put women on the margins of official religion, somewhat the way that Mother's Day eases women into a cul-de-sac of the contemporary American calendar. It is fine to celebrate mothers, as it was fine for the medieval Chinese of Hangchow to celebrate the ripening of the moon as a tribute to women—as long as these celebrations do not become the only feminine impress on the mythology running the general culture.

Traditional China was fiercely patriarchal, putting women in a place distinctly inferior to that of men. Present-day American culture, for all its pretense to sexual equality, has yet to work out symbolisms that make women as median, as much the norm, as men. Women still tend to stand on pedestals or in the gutter, while men occupy the level ground that shapes daily reality. If the majority of festivals in medieval China traded in symbols favoring men, the festival of the September moon had to carry a bittersweet taste. The same with our current celebration of Mother's Day.

The great challenge to men and women wanting sexual equality is to fashion an official culture (the one conferring status) that takes women into account as fully as men. When the official culture, the workaday world, the daily conception of self-identity and reality, is nearly unthinkingly male, no special festivals are going to compensate either women or the general populace for the huge loss that women's second-class status entails.

In saying this, I assume that the ideal culture solicits women's contributions as enthusiastically as men's and benefits from women's contributions as richly as from men's. This ideal is a complicated matter, because women are being solicited, and are contributing, all the time, even in distinctly unideal situations. For example, even when women are staffing the lower-paying jobs and making the volunteer organizations go, they are molding the general culture considerably. The problem is getting distinctly feminine experience and wisdom into the boardrooms of power where the agendas of the official culture are set. Until politicians come not merely to tolerate but actually to desire women's contributions, because they realize that women often see things that men do not, politics will never be fully healthy. The same with higher education, the life of the church, what goes on in the arts, and even what goes on in the sciences.

The ground-level symbolism that creation has given us is that both male and female humanity, creativity, intelligence, and fertility are necessary for the physical continuance and flourishing of the race. The upper-level lesson is that this both-and continues to operate in the spiritual order. We will not have a fully human church life, for instance, until we grant women leadership equal to that of men. We will not reform higher education until women shape the crucial decisions as much as men.

To the end of achieving such a time, the reality seems to be that we have to encourage three kinds of collaboration. Men have to interact in all-male groups, to bring out the creativity that male friendships and competitions stimulate. Women have to interact in all-female groups, to bring out the creativity that female bondings and sharings stimulate. And men and women have to interact in mixed company, with the crucial difference (from the patterns that prevail at present) that men not dominate women and women not have to accommodate to men.

It is not enough simply to create more situations in which men and women sit together in boardrooms or other places of power, influence, or impact. That is a start, but we shall accomplish the full task only when we get, because we welcome and sustain, the distinctive contributions of women. At the present, we lack these distinctive contributions. They do not exist in sufficient force to balance men's contributions, help correct the stereotypical deficiencies of men's contributions, and enrich society at large with the full creativity of its women. Overall, in any accurate calculation of how popular culture finally works, it is clear than women and men each contribute half. But for the matter of official, higher, dominant cultural patterns, we have yet to let or force women to contribute a full half. Indeed, we can barely imagine what a truly egalitarian culture would be like.

So, as we take pleasure in the scene of the festival for the fifteenth day of the eighth month in medieval Hangchow, we have to remember the pathos in such celebrations. Without focusing on this pathos so narrowly that we lose the ability to celebrate, we have to sense how underappreciated women have been in most traditional cultures. This can make us grateful for the progress that women have made in the developed countries in recent decades, but it can also make us marvel at how much remains to be done.

At what point will the moon become as significant as the sun? At what point will we become sophisticated enough to let each sex be itself and not close off huge zones of its creativity. The majority of women have yet to know, perhaps even suspect, how much they could do and be, if they stood alongside men at the centers of politics, religion, education, science, the arts, and the other great organs of our culture. The majority still feel that their creativity is linked with that of the moon, their bodies, their receptivity of male enlightenment and creativity. So the majority should think of the Chinese women celebrating the moon in the mid-September of a year toward the end of the thirteenth century as soul sisters—an ambiguous, bittersweet thought.

TARA

In a piece entitled "The Cry of Suffering to Tara" we read, "From my heart I bow to the Holy Lady, essence of compassion, the three unerring and precious places of refuge gathered into one; until I gain the terrace of enlightenment I pray you grasp me with the hook of your compassion. From the depth of my inmost heart and bones I pray to you (the Three Jewels bear witness this is not just from my mouth): think of me a little, show me your smiling face, loving one! Grant me the nectar of your voice."[7]

This piece comes from Tibetan Buddhism. It was composed by a lama, a Tibetan Buddhist monk. Tara is the most significant Tibetan Buddhist deity, a benevolent mother goddess. The best analogue, among the mythical figures of women that we have studied thus far, is the Prajnaparamita. But the tone is different here. Even though Tibetan Buddhism drew much from the Mahayana philosophy that underwrote the worship of the Prajanaparamita, it added a distinctive reliance on the imagination. Tara is a more powerful mandala of ultimate reality than the Prajnaparamita. The iconography of her maternal concern is lusher, more central to mainstream devotion. Here an intellectual renders her the focus of the basic truths of Buddhist faith. In other places peasant people approached her as the gracious Queen of Heaven, who could grant their petitions, heal their wounds, help them through their so many troubles.

The lama bows to the Holy Lady. He is the petitioner, the subject; she is the one who can grant petitions, the majesty. In bowing low, he renders homage with his body. He is small. She is great. He is the child, the peasant, the servant. She is the mother, the queen, the ruler. Compassion is the premier Buddhist virtue. If the first Buddhist truth is "All life is suffering," the first kindly response to this truth is "Be compassionate toward all living (suffering) things."

The Mahayana saint (bodhisattva) vowed to postpone entry into nirvana until the salvation of all living things had come to pass. As long as one sentient creature continued to be imprisoned in samsara, the realm of karmic bondage and so suffering, the saint could not enjoy the bliss of unconditionedness (freedom from all karmic constraints). So to call Tara the essence of compassion is to establish a powerful dialectical imagery. She is the personification of what is quintessential about Buddhist virtue and holiness. In turn, compassion is what Tara shows her petitioners—she defines what compassion is like.

To say that Tara is the three unerring and precious places of refuge gathered into one is to focus in her all the virtue and strength of the Buddha, the Dharma (Teaching), and the Sangha

(Community). These are the three jewels of Buddhism, the three places where those vowing to follow the Way of the Enlightened One take refuge. All people need refuge, because all life is suffering. The achievement of the Buddha was to understand the nature of suffering and so be able to prescribe how to stop it. The achievement of the Dharma was to articulate this understanding, giving it full form and elaborating it doctrinally. The achievement of the community that the Buddha established was to give the Way a social body. From the Sangha earnest disciples could gain wise teachers, noble exemplars, a channel for ongoing tradition.

Each of these three jewels made a distinctive contribution to the treasury of Buddhist faith. None of them was dispensable. So to focus all of them on Tara was to make her the epitome of the entire Buddhist pathway. In her adhered the very substance of enlightenment, wisdom, and communal support. Those who came to her wholeheartedly could find everything that the profession of Buddhist faith sought and required.

The terrace of enlightenment is the petitioner's, the devotee's, personal experience of how all life is suffering, the cause of suffering is desire, and the cessation of desire is the removal of suffering. When the disciple replicates the experience of Gautama, becoming flooded with light as he was, the disciple gains the substance of nirvana—escape from the realm of karmic suffering, entrance upon the freedom and fulfillment of unconditionedness. Gaining this terrace, this state, might take many lifetimes. Buddhism accepted from pre-Buddhist Indian culture the notion of transmigration. The gist of the human being (not a self, but the tie of the different "heaps" composing the "person") moved after death. Depending on one's karma, good or bad, one moved into a new existence, above or below what one had enjoyed in one's prior existence. This was a painful process, the very essence of samsara. To have repeatedly to die and be reborn defined the pathos of karmic existence and so showed the pressing need for enlightenment and nirvana. One who had penetrated this reality, through intense meditation (to which lamas were exposed and held) could cry out to Tara with genuine emotion. Existing apart from the terrace of enlightenment was sore pain.

The hook of Tara's compassion was her reaching out to help her devotee. Moved by the sight of the petitioner's sufferings, she could bind him or her to herself. The Buddhist store of faith held that the Buddha was "skillful in means" to save all suffering beings. Enlightenment gave Gautama, and the many other Buddhas, the wisdom to mediate help to all creatures, regardless of their situations. Here Tara is assumed to have this great power. She is treated as a powerful Buddha, an embodiment of the perfection that has left samsara behind yet knows how to help those still entrapped in it. If she hooks her compassion into the condition of the petitioner, all will become well. If she does not, the petitioner will continue to languish and suffer.

The assurance that this petition comes from the inmost heart and bones suggests a monastic context, where petition was a regular, daily event. People who meditate or pray every day face the problem of routinization. The rituals they go through, the prayers they are required to recite, can become rote, formalistic. Again and again, they have to renew the inner feeling that the prayers are supposed to express. Again and again they have to muster spiritual dispositions to match outer words, lest they become hypocrites.

Buddhism had arisen as a negative reaction to the formalism of Brahmanic (priestly) Hinduism. The Buddha had observed that many prayers and sacrifices did not guarantee wisdom or holiness. To find enlightenment, personal liberation, he had to take a different pathway. So, even when Buddhism established its own monastic routines, something lingered from the original rebellion of Gautama. At the least, this lama recognizes that he may have to convince Tara that he is not merely mouthing words. She hears so many petitions each day; why should she listen to his? What in his entreaties ought to prompt her to grab him with the hook of compassion? His soul-deep sincerity, he says. He means what he says, and he calls the Three Jewels to witness. This may also have been a familiar formula, but even so, it remained sacrosanct. In effect he is saying that he swears by all that is holy, all that lodges in the inner sanctums of Buddhism, that he means what he says.

The final request is modest, as though the petitioner is reminded of his humble status. It is also cunning, calculated to appeal to a maternal or even romantic feminine deity. He asks only that the Goddess think of him a little. The implication, like that of a chivalric knight, is that he is languishing in his love for her. The slightest acknowledgment will mean the world to him. Alternately, he is the small child who always has a claim on his mother's heart. He knows that she is supposed to think of him always because she has given him life. So to ask her to think of him a little is to play on her guilt. She is supposed to be ever on the watch for his well-being. To think of him a little and grant his petition is so small a boon that she ought to grant it quickly, unthinkingly.

To show the petitioner her shining face is for Tara to grant what he begs. She would not be smiling if she disapproved of his behavior. Her smiling face has to be beautiful, both in itself and to the devotee longing to see it. That can be assumed. So the prayer is flattering, close to the ingratiation of the lover. Tara is considered a female glad to be told she has a lovely smile. It has to please her that someone, an admirer, wants to bask in the glow of her acknowledgment. If she would further condescend to speak, the petitioner's cup would overflow. Her voice is like nectar, the liquor of the gods. Such a "speaking" might be an inner illumination, real progress toward enlightenment. Or it might be a feeling of being accepted, encouraged, or warmed to keep striving. The addresses of the deities are not limited to prosaic speeches. By calling her "loving one," the petitioner asks her to remember her own better nature. Part of her office is to punish evildoers and so defend justice and righteousness. But the better part is to show love, support, and help to the good, those striving to walk the Way generously. The petitioner therefore implies that he is trying hard and ought to be numbered among the good. Needy though he remains, he still merits her love because she "must" warm toward those trying to do what is right.

Written by a male, this prayer shows how the female images of mother, queen, figure of wisdom, muse, and even lover can combine in the male religious imagination when it seeks help in petitioning ultimate reality and supporting its hopes that ultimate reality is on its side. Because the vast majority of Asian religious literature has been written or edited by men, we find this view of female divinity frequently. In contrast, although the vast majority of Western religious literature has also been written or edited by men, we do not find this view of female divinity in the West.

The difference seems to flow from the relatively ahistorical character of Asian theology. Asian theology has not been tied to time and place, an original cultural conditioning, so self-consciously as the Jewish, Christian, and Muslim theologies have been. These latter views of ultimate reality have retained their umbilical ties to the patriarchal cultures in which they arose. Moreover, they have insisted that what happened to Abraham and Moses, Jesus and Paul, Muhammad and the communities of Mecca and Medina established patterns normative for all subsequent time. In those Western beginnings, God was a patriarch, and female sacredness was suspect. Thus we have had little petition of female divinity in the Western mainstream. On the sidelines, where images of the lovely Torah or the Virgin Mary flourished, sacredness has been feminine. But the comptrollers of the official accounting made sure that such sacredness stayed peripheral, symbolic rather than literal or dogmatic.

Nonetheless, the Tibetan Buddhist imagery can remind women, and men, of the possibilities that emerge when one does not constrain ultimate reality to masculinity. Taking seriously the unobjectionable proposition that divinity is beyond all sexual characterization or limitation, one can imagine healthy Western equivalents of the Tibetan approach to Tara. Westerners could pray to God the Mother as easily as God the Father. They could petition the divine mercy on the model of a child lisping its needs to the one who gave it birth and nursing. All this would become possible, if we allowed the mythical character of Asian theology to make its proper impact on our understanding of Western theology. For those feeling the need of a feminine persona in God, the liberation could be considerable.

DOUBLE BINDS

Hindu mythology is especially rich in sexual themes, including those of male-female antagonism among the deities. An important stratum of myths about the gods makes the Great Goddess the original source of all later deities. Other stories derive female goddesses from male. The overall result is a standoff. Even when patriarchal influences conspire to place femininity below masculinity, important evidence remains to counter this tendency and suggest how femininity is superior or more primordial.

Like Greek mythology, that of India has its share of encounters between divinities and mortals. On the whole, female mortals have a tougher time than male finessing such encounters. In some situations, the females seemed damned if they do and damned if they don't. The double standard that makes it legitimate for males to be licentious but insists that females be chaste appears frequently. Indeed, the females can find themselves in the position of being condemned if they succumb to unchaste overtures from the gods and punished if they fight back. This is the situation in the following story from the popular Purana literature of South India: "One day, when the Rishi [sage] was away from home, the Trimurti [Brahma, Visnu, and Siva] came to visit her [Anasuya, the sage's wife], to see whether she was as beautiful and virtuous as reported. Not knowing who they were, and resenting their intrusion, she had them changed into little children. They naturally took offense, and cursed her, so that her beauty faded away, and her face became dotted with marks like those of the smallpox."[8]

The customary intepretation of this visit is that the gods wanted to have sexual experience of Anasuya—if need be, by rape. She had sufficient power (either in her own right or as the wife of a sage) to thwart their advances. They were humiliated to be turned into children, but this change had served Anasuya's purposes, because it had removed their sexual threat without destroying them. In turning against her, they said, in effect, "If we can't have your beauty, no one shall." The curse by smallpox was unfair, but who can constrain the gods? The ominous implication in the depths of the story is that women can never expect to receive justice. If Anasuya had succumbed to their advances, she would have been liable to the heavy charge of having been unfaithful to her husband. What he might have done to her, or what the gods themselves might have decreed as punishment, she could not know.

The story tells us that Anasuya did not recognize the three great gods as divinities. Perhaps that was part of their pique. But even if she had recognized them, her moral dilemma would have remained, for how could she have honored them as gods and credited them with immoral intentions? In doing that, she would have shattered the entire basis of the moral order, establishing immorality in the precincts of heaven. In fact, the story forces us to conclude that heaven may be immoral.

Still, we have to admire Anasuya's resistance to such a thought. Indeed, we have to wonder whether we are not to conclude that the virtue of mortals can exceed that of the gods, and so realize that the upright human conscience is the last court of moral judgment. What we are to do with the fact that honoring her upright human conscience brought Anasuya painful affliction is not clear. The story itself is amoral, if not immoral. The flexibility of the Hindu scriptural canon allows us to cast this tradition outside the borders of what was considered normative, but this cannot disguise the fact that many South Indians could be taken in. We have to hope that the overall

configuration of the tales they considered sacred counterbal-
anced this one, but we have also to suspect that, when it came
to protecting the moral rights and reputations of women, those
who expounded the scriptures could be less than zealous.

Hinduism is fascinating precisely because of inner contradictions such as this. Sometimes it strikes the comparativist as the
greatest museum of religious imagery—a vast living collection
generated by the principle that nothing ought to be kept out.
Still, while one finds many stories promoting the virtues of the
Goddess and many stories extolling the merits of the virtuous
wife and mother, the total slant of Hindu tradition greatly subor-
dinates women to men and is not averse to putting women in
double binds. The epitome of the Hindu attitude toward women
has been the proposition that women cannot gain *moksha* (enlightenment, liberation, salvation—the Hindu equivalent of the
Buddhist nirvana). To gain moksha, a woman has to be reborn
as a man. Only from existence as a man (usually of the upper
classes) can one break the karmic bonds that keep one in samsara. Existence as a woman is evidence that one's karmic status
is woefully low, and so one's chances for moksha are virtually
nil. Perhaps this judgment made it legitimate to place women
in no-win situations. Perhaps only men merited a fully fair moral
treatment.

A story of the contemporary French writer Marguerite Yourcenar about the goddess Kali seems to proceed from this premise.
Kali has been thrown out of heaven for unspecified offenses
(probably, we suspect, for simply being herself: the grim avenger,
the unwelcome reminder of death). Her punishment has been
to wander in time as a prostitute. Terribly weary, and on the
verge of hating creation (wondering why the gods ever made a
world), she meets a wise man who, simply in virtue of being
male, presumes to instruct her, though in a kindly tone:

The Master of Great Compassion lifted a hand to bless the passing woman. "My immaculate head has been fixed to the body of
infamy," she said. "I desire and do not desire, I suffer and yet I

enjoy, I loathe living and am afraid to die." "We are all incomplete," said the wise man. "We are all pieces, fragments, shadows, matterless ghosts. We all have believed that we have wept and that we have felt pleasure for countless centuries." . . . "I am tired," moaned the goddess. Then touching with the tip of his finger the black tresses soiled with ashes, he said: "Desire has taught you the emptiness of desire; regret has shown you the uselessness of regret. Be patient, Error of which we are all a part. Imperfect creature thanks to whom perfection becomes aware of itself, O Lust which is not necessarily immortal."[9]

The story has so many inner contradictions that it seems to capture the impossible situation in which all mortal creatures, but especially women, often find themselves. The goddess has wanted to be herself, but for that she has been forced into infamy. Prostitution is a primordial symbol for debasement, the corruption of the best into the worst. She moans with fatigue and self-division. The sage wants to move to the general condition of mortal beings, our universal state of incompleteness. Yet Kali remains more than a generalization. Her black tresses tinged with ashes specify the conflicted beauty that mortal women often manifest. Has she indeed experienced the emptiness of everything, or has she been emptied against her will—so violated by others that she is weary of being herself?

There is no indication that her imperfections have made Kali aware of perfection. There is no indication that she merits being called Lust with a capital L. She did not choose her status as a prostitute, and any desire she has for this status is outweighed by her moral fatigue. So it is diminished comfort to hear that her self, standing for Lust, may not be immortal, that it also will pass. Her self has become what it is, loathsome in her sight, because she has been forced into the archetypal abuse inflicted on women. The warped views of both the gods and human cultures have placed her in an impossible situation. Mythical woman that she is, she cannot get out of the story that others have written for her. Poor, lovely, bedraggled goddess, her cold comfort is the woolly nostrums of male commentators. Surely

all women chafing under patriarchal religious regimes can sympathize with this Kali. Surely their hearts must go out to her and
hate her bondage. And surely they must see that, but for the
grace of a better divinity, her many binds could be their own.

LAKSMI

Laksmi, wife of the Hindu God Visnu, illustrates the Hindu
tendency to make any divine focus comprehensive. When they
considered the virtues or functions of any god or goddess long
enough, devotees tended to credit him or her with all the powers
of unrestricted divinity. Thus Laksmi, who often appears to be
merely a goddess of good fortune, the source of material blessings, was taken by the Pancaratra school of philosophy to be the
foremost principle of creation. David Kinsley has described the
process by which this happened:

In the Pancaratra school, Laksmi comes to play the central role
in the creation and evolution of the universe as the *sakti* [female
consort and energy] of Visnu. In the Pancaratra creation scenario
Visnu remains almost entirely inactive, relegating the creative
process to Laksmi. After awakening Laksmi at the end of the
night of dissolution [the period when the cosmos goes into chaos,
before reemerging into ordered creation], Visnu's role in the creation of the universe is restricted to that of an inactive architect
whose plan is put into effect by a builder. Laksmi alone acts,
and the impression throughout the cosmogony is that she acts
independently of Visnu, although it is stated that she acts according to his wishes.

The practical effect of Visnu's inactive role in creation is that
he becomes so aloof that Laksmi dominates the entire Pancaratra
vision of the divine. In effect, she acquires the position of the
supreme divine principle, the underlying reality upon which all
rests, that which pervades all creation with vitality, will, and
consciousness. The *Laksmi-tantra*, a popular Pancaratra text, says
that Laksmi undertakes the entire stupendous creation of the

universe with only one-billionth of herself (14.3). So transcendent is she, so beyond the ability of the mind to circumscribe her, that only a miniscule fraction of her is manifest in the creation of the universe. Elsewhere in the same text she describes herself as follows: "Inherent in the (principle of) existence, whether manifested or unmanifested, I am at all times the inciter (potential element of all things). I manifest myself (as the creation), I ultimately dissolve myself (at the time of destruction) and I occupy myself with activity (when creation starts functioning). I alone send (the creation) forth and (again) destroy it. I absolve the sins of the good. As the (mother) earth towards all beings, I pardon them (all their sins). I mete everything out. I am the thinking process and I am contained in everything" (50.65.67). Functionally, Laksmi has taken over the cosmic tasks of the three great male gods of the Hindu pantheon: Brahma, Visnu, and Siva.[10]

For our purposes, the key notion is the ability of female divinity to expand to the point where it takes over all the functions of divinity itself, even though divinity itself tends to be considered more male than female. The Hindu trinity is a threesome of male gods: Brahma is the Creator, Visnu is the Preserver, and Siva is the Destroyer. Here we find Laksmi moving from the role of consort of Visnu to that of Creator-Preserver-Destroyer. Certainly, this illustrates the Hindu intuition that distinctions among the functions of the deities, or even among the identities of the deities, are matters of convenience more than strict ontology. The gods do not stand apart from one another in being. Given the slightest provocation, they meld, taking over one another's attributes and functions. Here reflection on the basic dualism of masculine and feminine divinity has begun a process that ends with Laksmi standing for divinity as such.

The basic dualism of masculine and feminine divinity, as the mainstream of classical Hindu philosophical speculation pictured it, was the passivity of the male deity and the energetic activity of the female deity. Paired as husband and wife, even represented iconographically as an androgyne, these two aspects of divinity had a rank of superior and inferior. Probably under the influence of yogic love of self-control ("enstasis," Mircea Eliade has called it), many meditative philosophers pictured the superior male deity as composed, self-possessed, above action or energy, which might dissipate the self. In contrast, and for the sake of completion, the inferior female deity was pictured as aroused, fiery, full of passionate energy. She was the *sakti*, the creative force of the male deity, necessary to bring change about, including the momentous change of creation, but dangerous and always in need of his control. This stereotype wrote large the prejudice that women are more emotional and volatile than men, more passionate and liable to act impetuously. Here we see the logical conclusion of this initial depiction of the two kinds of divinity. Visnu has become so passive, so removed from the world of creation, that Laksmi has had to step in and control the whole process. By the end, she is the comprehensive divinity, making the universe run and offering human beings the forgiveness they so desperately need.

Hinduism seldom conceived of creation as from nothingness. Usually creation was an endless process of expansion and contraction. It had no beginning, and it would have no end. It proceeded in pulsations of great length sometimes referred to as Brahma days and Brahma nights. The days were the times of light and creativity; the nights were the times of darkness and dissolution. Here Laksmi presides over both—the entire pulsation. Furthermore, she is like the other creators in furnishing the substance of creation from herself. Everything that comes to be does so out of her being. Her being is so vast that the entire world amounts to only one-billionth of her substance. Still, since it is from her, she is in it. One can even say that she is it: the world is a form of her. In its ultimate reality and identity, the world is she. Certainly, we find texts making similar statements about other divinities. In the Bhagavad Gita, for example, creation is depicted as the expression of Krishna. In the final analysis, everything is he, and he is everything. The difficulty with this conception, wherever found, is that the world can lose its reality: only the divinity expressed in the world is truly or fully real. The advantage is that everything can bear divinity to the believer, can be a focus in which the believer can find divinity, worship it, and so advance toward moksha.

The distinctive logic riveting this metaphysical cast of mind onto Laksmi has two peculiar moments. First, as we have noted, the beginning of the possibility of her taking over the whole of creation is her energetic complementing of the passive Visnu, her consort. Second, when it becomes clear that she is going to be the whole of creation, a motif of motherhood appears. In thinking about how she sends forth creation, the authors of the text instinctively picture her as mother earth, the bountiful womb. Interestingly, they then move to a theme of forgiveness, as though thinking of her as a mother inevitably leads to think-ing of her as pardoning the sins of the good. The tacit middle premise is that the good are her children. Naturally, then, she will see to their benefits, the greatest of which is forgiving them their sins (freeing them of their karmic burdens, and so preparing them for moksha).

The most interesting implication that I find in this philosophi-cal expansion of the significance of Laksmi is an intuition that femininity is equiprimordial with masculinity. I do not read this text as a specimen of feminist triumphalism. Too many other texts do similar things with male gods to allow us to think that Laksmi is unique in coming to stand for the whole of the divine control of creation. So, sufficient is the evidence that femininity could be as divine, as comprehensive, as valid a beginning and ending point for speculation about the grounds and causes of creation as masculinity. Laksmi ends as the equivalent of the Hindu Trinity. Sacral femininity can explain creation, preserva-tion, and destruction, just as well as sacral masculinity can. In the final analysis, maleness and femaleness are equally transpar-ent for divinity. Neither form or mask has a definitive advantage or priority. Male fertility is no more potent or self-sufficient than female. Male ways are no more godly than female ways. Obviously, the cultural implications of this confession are enormous.

Inasmuch as divinity grounds a given culture, it provides the ultimate sanctions for the images regnant in that culture. Logically, then, a divinity thoroughly bisexual, equally expressible through male or female forms and images, should ground a culture in which to be male or female is finally irrelevant, because the sexes are considered equally human. Obviously, this has not been the case in the vast majority of cultures, Hinduism emphatically included.

Virtually everywhere, the Pauline Christian intuition (Gal. 3:28) that "in Christ there is neither male nor female" (i.e., in the final, most sacred analysis, sex does not matter) has been honored only in the breech. Certainly that has been true in Christian cultures. Nonetheless, something of immense psychological significance, benefit, and health lies ready to hand in imagery such as that of the Christian Paul and the Hindu Pancaratra. Laksmi, like the ideal vision of the church, says that divinity—truly holy and ultimate reality—cannot be sexist. Against the stories that would make the Hindu Trinity oppressive toward women (for instance, the story of its abuse of Anasuya), this view of divinity makes it wholly congenial toward women—feminine to the core. In Hinduism one has always to pick one's version of the sacred truth, but at least symbolism like that of the creative Laksmi gives one the chance to avoid sexist versions. If the thinking process itself can be a female deity and the deity contained in everything can be feminine, then women can feel as rooted in ultimate reality, as dignified by ultimate reality, as their husbands and fathers, their brothers and lovers—an experience that could improve all their relationships.

4

Near Eastern Cultures

INANNA

In this chapter we deal with mythical femininity derived from the ancient Near East. The geographic designation is merely a matter of convenience, not something hard and fast. We shall consider Sumerian, Egyptian, Gnostic, Jewish, Christian, and Muslim images for divine femininity. All look back to the ancient Near East for their cultural beginnings, but the Jewish, Christian, and Muslim images have traveled widely, both to the West and farther East. Still, this grouping makes for an interesting comparison with the Asian mythology that we have seen. On the whole, the originally Near Eastern mythology of women is less philosophical and abstract, more vegetative and personal. Numerous distinctions clamor for attention, but such a first comparison can launch our inquiry.

Inanna, the ancient Sumerian goddess of fertility and prosperity, was paired with her consort Dumuzi during the ritual celebrated each New Year's Day. The people would construct a nuptial suite for the sacred couple, whose sexual union was thought necessary if the year to come was to be fertile. The song for the entry of the goddess and god into the nuptial suite included the following frank verses:

The queen bathes her holy loins, Inanna bathes for the holy loins of Dumuzi, She washes herself with soap. She sprinkles sweet-smelling cedar oil on the ground. The king goes with lifted head to the holy loins, Dumuzi goes with lifted head to the holy loins of Inanna. He lies down beside her on the bed. Tenderly he caresses her, murmuring words of love: "O my holy jewel! O my wondrous Inanna!" After he enters her holy vulva, causing the queen to rejoice, after he enters her holy vulva, causing Inanna to rejoice, Inanna holds him to her and murmurs, "O Dumuzi, you are truly my love." The king bids the people enter the great hall. The people bring food offerings and bowls. They burn juniper resin, perform laving rites, and pile up sweet-smelling incense. The king embraces his beloved bride, Dumuzi embraces Inanna. Inanna, seated on the royal throne, shines like daylight. The king, like the sun, shines radiantly by her side. He arranges abundance, lushness, and plenty before her. He assembles the people of Sumer. The musicians play for the queen. . . . They play songs for Inanna to rejoice the heart.[1]

Several motifs deserve comment. First, the obvious assimilation of the human queen to Inanna and the human king to Dumuzi reminds us of the mythical character of ancient Near Eastern culture as a whole. The gods above were the models for the conduct of life on earth below. The king and queen on earth had to fit themselves to the stories of Dumuzi and Inanna, the divine royalty. Indeed, on ritual occasions they had to personify the divine royalty. Second, the manifest concern was for fertility. The coupling of the royal pairs was necessary for the fruitful functioning of the cosmos. There was no doubt where the crux of prosperity lay. The vulva of Inanna, the womb of the cosmos, had to be healthy, well functioning, if the people, their animals, and their crops were to be fruitful and productive. Hence, third, the great solicitude was to please Inanna. The happier her vulva, the more prosperous the world would be. She had to be loved tenderly, shown full appreciation. It was important that her afterglow be like bright daylight. Fourth and last, the joy of Inanna flowed out to the entire people. Pleasing her, offering her the full celebration of a wedding feast, the people could enter joyously into the music, the eating, and the dancing, with the sense that the coming year would go well.

One can see why the Israelite prophets would be troubled by the fertility religion of the Canaanites, from whom they were trying to wrest cultural as well as physical control of the Promised Land. The Canaanite divinities functioned as the older Sumerian divinities had. Their coupling expressed the wedding of male and female powers necessary to make nature productive. Sex was a holy force, pervading the cosmos. Certainly it had its personal aspects (the poem for the Sumerian New Year festival is remarkably tender), but in the first place it was the objective economy of nature. Agriculture and animal husbandry depended on it. In the light of the fertility of nature as a whole, human sexuality seemed both casual and sacred. In sexual interaction, men and women were doing nothing more than what all animals did. What they were doing, however, was the very mechanism for transmitting life, and so it was mysterious, uniquely important—in a word, "sacred."

The Israelite prophets drew on a different sense of both nature and human beings. Because of the experiences associated with Abraham and Moses, their mental construction of the cosmos made it the free work of a divinity standing beyond it. All proper order came from acknowledging the unique sovereignty of this world-transcendent deity. To become embroiled in the fertility of nature was to miss the crucial point of both Israelite history and human nature. The one Lord was the only true divinity. Gods and goddesses who coupled for the fertilization of the earth were an abomination. Not only did they obscure the true reality and holiness of the one Lord, they also distracted people from a pure cult and put their brains in their loins. It was fine to respect the place of the loins in procreation, whether human or animal. It was sacrilegous, and so disgusting, to worship sexuality—hymn it, enact it ritually, beg sex-soaked goddesses and gods for favors.

The very intensity of the Israelite prophets' polemic against the fertility divinities of the Canaanites and their other neighbors suggests that the new theology was not obvious. Even the prophets' own people were beguiled by the natural forces of fertility. Again and again they took up what the prophets considered to be a false cult. Again and again their need to be assured that their family line would continue, their animals would increase, their crops would burgeon made the fertility goddesses and gods attractive. When one adds the seductions of human sexuality, the beguiling byplay and pleasure of human lovers, one realizes that the prophets were contending against an immensely powerful force.

Fateful indeed for later history was the prophets' agreement with the ancient Sumerians that female fertility was the crux of the entire matter. Where the ancient Sumerians sang hymns to the sacred vulva, however, the prophets made femininity womanhood, the special enemy of the transcendent religion they held so dear. Certainly ancient Sumer, like the rest of ancient Mesopotamia, had its own patriarchal patterns.[2] We should not think that a near-fixation on natural fertility made ordinary women queens at home. But in biblical Israel the wanton woman became the special symbol of religious infidelity. Whenever Israel defaulted on the covenant, the prophets pictured her as a harlot, an adulterous wife. Their imagery was not so frank as that of the Sumerian ritual for New Year's Day, but it did not avoid physical sex. Wanton Israel was like a female in heat. Going over to the gods of nature was giving to idols the desire properly reserved for the Lord.

On her own terms, Inanna was nowhere near so offensive. Grant that her people knew little of a transcedent God, a Creator who made the world independently and stood apart from it, running it as he (the Israelite Creator was male) chose, and you can find little reason to fault them. No doubt on occasion they fell into excessive veneration of fertility and so sexuality. No doubt the loins are not the highest human parts. But ancient Sumerians, as all other estimable peoples, knew this truth and honored it, in their own ways. When they carried out their fertility rites and apotheosized female sexuality, they were caring for the fundamentals of existence. At other times, in other ways, they could care for higher stages of existence: reflection, thought, worship, even love detached from sexual desire. Still, the mainstream of their culture tended to avoid the dualisms of both ancient Israel and classical Greece. Their basic instinct was to hold the world and divinity together, and to hold matter and spirit together as well.

That instinct is both the liability of the cosmological cultures (those that join nature and Divinity) and their great asset. They tend to lack the far reaches of spiritual ambition, attainment, and revelation that we find in Israel and Greece, but they do keep their feet planted solidly in the ground, stay fascinated with life and death, the ancient instructors in wisdom.[3] If their minds do not reach full clarity about thought (the nature of the mind itself), and their spirits do not receive the divine revelation that establishes self-sacrificing love as the best index of God, neither do they become fanatics, crazies, people who lose the world. So their balance tells us something that remains instructive, even after we have bowed low in gratitude to the Greeks who clarified reason and the Israelites who clarified divine love. That something is the centrality of symbolism, especially that of human sexuality, and its roots in the human body. The body has wisdoms that the Greek mind, and even the Israelite prophetic heart, does not know. And these wisdoms are especially significant for women.

Women are the more embodied, sensual sex. That is the cross-cultural stereotype, and as long as women are the ones who give birth, they will be forced to carry it. Women know about life and death more somatically than men, even though men are fully embodied. Women's experience of time is cyclic, as long as they menstruate. As long as they are smaller than men, more delicate, more easily bruised and wounded, women will be more expert than men about the fragility of life. Childbearing and childrearing only deepen and broaden this expertise. Sexual experience only brings it to bear on pleasure, suggesting that behind the festal songs of ancient Sumer lay considerable irony, even pathos. The pleasures of love are fragile, often fleeting. One cannot overlook for long the consequences of love, and its demanding conditions. Inasmuch as the ancient Sumerian veneration of female fertility carried great potential for wisdom about concrete, fully embodied human love, it continues to be a stratum of human experience that we are wise to mine.

Every time that we abuse women, especially through sexual crimes, we show how terribly ignorant we are. Every time that we find ourselves shaped by degrading stereotypes of women, we can suspect the limits, the liabilities, in our own cultural heritage from Greece and Israel. And every time that we treat the earth as less than a sacred goddess, a never-failing source of wonder because a great mystery of fertility, we show our need of rites and instructions like those celebrated for Inanna. If we wished, she could become a patroness of ecology. Her potential for doing us good is far from exhausted by taking her frank sexuality to heart. We have a great deal yet to learn about the ties between female embodiment and the future health of mother earth.

ISIS

In ancient Egypt, where goddesses were not simply variations on the fertility of mother earth (in fact, the Egyptian earth deity was male), Isis stands out as a great figure of wisdom. She was the wife and sister of Osiris, god of fertility and the underworld. She was the mother of the pharaoh, symbolized by the throne in which he sat. But perhaps most impressively, she was the source of wisdom about the divine creator, Re (the sun god). The story of how she gained this special status is instructive:

According to the religious conceptions of antiquity, real wisdom consisted of insight into the mystery of life and death. This knowledge is creative: it evokes life from death. Thus wisdom was to the Egyptians equivalent to the capacity of exerting magical power. Isis possessed this gift to a high degree. This appears, for instance, in a curious text relating how Isis obtained knowledge of the secret name of the god Re. It is well-known that in antiquity a name was considered to include the very nature of the person who bore the name. Thus the secret name of Re contained the mystery of his creative power. According to the myth, as Re grew old his mouth trembled and his spittle dropped on the ground. Isis mixed his spittle with a bit of earth and shaped a snake, which she placed on the path on which Re used to walk. When Re approached the snake bit him. Re cried out in pain, but he did not know what caused his illness. Isis, along with other deities, pitied him. She offered to cure him by her wisdom and her magic art on the condition that he would reveal his real name. Immediately, he listed a series of impressive names, but Isis was not deceived and insisted on knowing his secret name. Finally, Re was forced to comply with her demand and whispered his name in the ear of Isis so that nobody could hear the secret except the goddess. This myth means that the creator god is unknowable: Isis alone, the wise goddess, has insight into his being.[4]

In Hellenistic times, when the many religious cultures of the ancient Near East swam together with the Greek and Roman cultures, Isis became an important figure in the mystery religions—those pursuits of the meaning of life and death (and so of the way to immortality) with which Christianity eventually competed successfully. She served women as a symbol of both faithful love (her mourning for the dead Osiris became a paradigm) and creative motherhood (her sponsorship of the pharaoh, her son, also became a paradigm). But both of these stereotypically feminine functions derived from her signal wisdom. She had learned about death painfully, in searching for the pieces of the dismembered Osiris and bringing him back to life. And as this story tells us, she had used her magical powers to wrest from the great god Re the secret of his inmost identity. Devotees therefore could go to her with complete confidence. She was much more than a figure of female fertility. She stood for the creative wisdom by which birth and death could be managed:

understood, borne, and in some ways manipulated. The model she gave to Egyptian women was serene and self-confident. In her wisdom lay an attractive strength. The arts of healing and successful childbirth thrived under her patronage. She said that being female was a good way to gain access to the secrets of existence, the great dramas of life and death.

Consider the implication of this constellation of ideas. The heart of feminine significance may lie in wisdom about the central mystery of life and death. On one level, this observation seems banal. The heart of any human wisdom lies in penetrating beyond ordinary measure the central mystery of life and death. On another level, however, wisdom about the central mystery of life and death holds out the prospect of great independence and dignity. Isis is serene, untroubled, as though she knows her great worth. Certainly, she has power over the king, her son. Certainly, she is pleased to be an intimate of Re, the Sun, who makes everything happen, even though her intimacy may not please him. But she need not trade on these relationships. She does not have to throw her weight around, demonstrate her power. If she moves to help a devotee, it is from grace rather than political necessity. If she involves herself in the machinations that swirl around the throne, or around the cosmic decisions of Re, it is because she chooses to do so, not because she has to shore up her position. Her position is secure, in both her own eyes and the eyes of knowledgeable beholders, because of her competence. She knows. She is wise. No one can take that from her.

How far does the notion that wisdom, competence, is a secure basis for confidence and independence take us? Is it realistic to propose this notion to women, who often lament that they have no self-confidence, that they do not feel they are worth very much? Obviously, no blanket answer will be fully helpful, but perhaps thinking about the kinds of wisdom that women can realistically hope to acquire will be consoling.

Women in the professions are held to the same standards as their male counterparts, if not to higher ones. As lawyers, doctors, or professors, they have to perform well according to the going criteria of their guilds. Even though many such women carry greater burdens at home than their male counterparts, that cuts them no slack when it comes to evaluations, promotions, and pay raises. What they have to do as parents, spouses, and homemakers is largely irrelevant. From time to time some enlightened person suggests developing more sophisticated and compassionate models for evaluating professional work, but such models seldom get beyond the drawing board. In the university, for example, how a person publishes and teaches is the basis of decisions about tenure and promotion. Other, outside considerations may enter in, but the heart of the matter is always supposed to be published research and teaching.

I sympathize with those having to negotiate the cluster of problems surrounding objectivity and subjectivity in professional evaluations. Even though I would like to see women's social roles and obligations taken into account, I realize that it is hard to determine how they ought to be. But the sense of confidence that I find more important for women lies outside the approval of peers, professional or other. Few professional evaluations deal with wisdom, and all human beings, professional or not, need to gain wisdom, ought to be judged in terms of wisdom. What do I know about life and death? How do I understand the secrets of the creative force running the world? These are questions women might ask themselves profitably. My impression is that too few women raise these questions and that their failure to raise them (and find ways to answer them) frequently is tied to a sense of inadequacy.

Without discounting the enormous impact that social conditioning plays in people's sense of themselves, I believe that individuals have some independence from social roles. If, in their heart of hearts, any people feel good about human existence—have found a way to make sense of the world and keep themselves going—no social conditioning can enslave them. For my biases, religious contemplation is the royal road to such a desirable situation. In my experience, people who reflect and pray, so that they have personal experience of the mystery of existence, enter upon a peace that surpasses purely human understanding. They may never become serene, as Isis models serenity. They may never feel fully confident to negotiate their way in the world of commerce, medicine, law, or higher education. But they can come to feel confident that they know how to bring up their children and comfort them in the dark of night, when the children are sick or crying from a nightmare. They can come to a wonderful detachment from the vast amounts of vanity, false values, and plain foolishness that their contemporaries imbibe from the mass media. In quiet, helped by scriptural texts and serious conversations with good friends not afraid to wonder out loud about life and death, they can possess their souls, their most intimate selves.

This is the core of freedom, as I understand it. The wisdom of the world religions boils down to an otherworldly perspective. This does not mean flight from the world of children and money. It means finding ways to keep children, money, politics, church affairs, work, and everything else that is less than life and death from swelling up, gaining undue importance, and becoming an idol. The real wisdom for which we ought to labor is to know how things stand, order themselves, sift out "under the aspect of eternity." What do we realize is truly important when we look from the angle of our deathbed? What are we most concerned to give our children when they rest in our arms right after birth? And what does what we see, remember, and learn again by visiting such moments tell us about ourselves? Does it not say that if we know what is really important—love, honesty, unconditional support, integrity, fidelity in work and friendship—we need bow to no lesser gods? Egyptian mythology says that Isis, a prototypical female, learned from Re what was really important and that what she learned set her free. She became her own person. The truly liberating message would be that any of us daughters or sons of Isis can do the same.

Such a message explains why bars need not a prison make. Equally, it explains why many of the affluent exiting the shops on Rodeo Drive are pitiable. If they have not done what Isis did, have not measured what is really important by the criteria of creativity and mortality, life and death, they are of all of us the most to be pitied. Poor little rich kids, sad little celebrities, their lives can be much thinner than the lives of ordinary, unremarkable people who merely know how to read reflectively, how to taste the significance of well-tested texts.

Wisdom is savory. It tastes sweet to the soul. The more we draw nourishment from it, the greater our appetite for it becomes. Women are at least as apt for this savoriness as men. Women are at least as sensitive to the implications of their experience, as primed to store things up in their hearts and ponder them. If women tend to be outsiders, as the patriarchalism of most cultures ensures, they can see what is really important with a clarity that few insiders, few movers and shakers, can match. Detached, women have less ego to block their view and more need to find alternatives to what the crowd thinks, what the advertising industry wants to sell. Cultivating the part of her that warms to Isis, any present-day woman might be surprised by joy: there are no sexual, racial, or economic barriers to wisdom. There is no experience that cannot be mined profitably. Certainly, people have to be helped to reflection, as they have to be rescued from situations in which all experience seems painful, cruel, or hopeless. But on the whole, the conditions for wisdom are minimal. Simply by stepping aside and thinking things over, one can start to walk a pathway to self-confidence and independence. That is what Isis can teach present-day women: nothing need keep us from becoming wise, and so free.

THE GNOSTIC SOPHIA

The Gnostic movement, which was a powerful Mediterranean influence during the first centuries A.D., wove together many different sources. Greek philosophy and Jewish apocalyptic writings were influential, as were Egyptian and Manichean ideas.

This movement promised salvation in the sense of release from the imperfections of the current cosmic situation, which was fallen. Human beings now found themselves in a world less perfect than had been the case earlier, at the beginning, before the fall into matter and mortality. On the whole, the Gnostics did not think of this fall as sinful, in the way that the biblical authors spoke of sin. They did not postulate a willful revolt against a single Creator, responsible for the whole of existence. Rather, they were struggling to explain the painful limitations that reason runs into when it contemplates the human condition. The tension between what we want—complete satisfaction, perhaps even eternal fulfillment—and what our limitations allow, especially those consequent on our having bodies, suggested that "once upon a time" things had been better.

When they imagined how to understand the process from "once upon a time" to the present, many of the Gnostics focused on Wisdom, a personification or extrapolation of the knowledge by which the world runs. If one could get in contact with this Wisdom, one might escape from the prison of material creation and regain the blessed condition that ruled before the fall of spirit into matter. One such personification of Wisdom suggests the coexistence of male and female elements at the foundations of creation: "This is the First Thought, His image. She was the Mother of the All, because she was before them all, Mother-Father, First Man, Holy Spirit, triple male, triple power, triple male-female name, and eternal aeon of the invisible ones, and first to come forth."[5]

In her careful study of this and similar Gnostic texts, Pheme Perkins notes the theme that we found in the Egyptian Isis: behind all human wisdom lies a motherly figure, the source of saving knowledge. Just as Isis stood below Re, yet also could be more important than Re, in part because she knew his secret name, so the Gnostic Wisdom (Sophia) could focus the devotee's efforts to gain the knowledge necessary for salvation.

Thus, in concluding her study, Perkins writes:

The mythic summary of Sophia's wandering fits within the cultic proclamation of saving gnosis. That gnosis overcomes the ambiguities and tensions inherent in the Gnostic's experience of the world. *Thund's* [another Wisdom Goddess's] paradoxes intensify those experiences so as to overcome the disvaluing effect that they might have on the believer. Though the Mother/Sophia is not the highest Father or the only revealer of gnosis, she often appears as the crucial link between the human in this world and that divinity which constitutes his/her truest identity. The peculiar amalgamation of mythic and philosophic discourse suggests that her wisdom also provides a challenge to the claims of human reason advanced through philosophy. The ultimate image of salvation is neither male nor female but the restored unity of an androgynous Mother-Father, who has passed through diversity.[6]

We have noted the presence of gods and goddesses, male and female divinities, in such classically mythological cultures as the Hindu. There the overall message seemed to be that ultimate reality incorporates both sets of qualities, female as well as male. The same apparently held true for many of the classical Gnostics. Underneath their often complicated schemata of how the present, fallen world came to be lay an intuition that a primal unity had been lost and would have to be reacquired in the march to salvation. The philosophical sources of Gnosticism might suggest that divinity lay beyond contrasts or differentiations such as male and female. But the mythological needs of many Gnostics necessitated coming to grips with sexual imagery—reconciling male and female aspects of ultimate reality.

When they prayed to the great Sophia, the wisdom figure in whom the knowledge of salvation focused, the Gnostics expressed their longing for an all-knowing Mother. Even if this all-knowing Mother was subordinate to a creative Father, she remained indispensable. In fact, the comprehensive figure of divinity was an androgynous Mother-Father. The Gnostic rituals had to provide for this intuition. If the task was to picture the One who understood how the world functioned and could lead the wayward to salvation, to accomplish the task one needed a motherly Sophia as much as a fatherly creative Power.

Nowadays it can be difficult to speak of androgyny. Feminists can oppose making the sexes complementary, pointing to the history of women's subordination to men under that rubric. Advocates of men's rights can be equally independent, steering clear of any effort to say how the sexes need one another. So, beyond noting that male and female chromosomes are necessary for procreation, there is little one can say without fear of contradiction. As ideologues of several stripes will be quick to point out, we can cite social conditioning to demolish any claim that there are innately male or female traits, characteristics, virtues, or vices.

This is a powerful argument, and yet I sense that most people do not buy it. They may fear offending against the current orthodoxy, which fights any limitation that adjectives such as "female," "male," "gay," "straight," "handicapped," "aged," "African-American," "white," "poor," or "middle-class" might conjure up. Yet they know that to negotiate everyday affairs at work, when shopping, in church, in dealing with children, and a dozen other places, they have to work with stereotypes or generalizations about the differences between the sexes. The Gnostic way to handle such experience was to suggest that, in the final analysis, all significant sexual characteristics have their place. Ultimate reality itself, divinity, provides for all. If one wishes, then, one can use a given understanding of sexual differences with theological impunity. The Mother Sophia can provide salvation as surely as the Father Creator.

Is this indeed another species of wisdom, freedom, and liberation that we should cherish? Are there ways to consider women physically weaker than men, more emotional (and so perhaps more human) than men, more intuitive than men, more refined than men, less self-reliant and individualistic than men, less divided and less angry, that impose none of these characteristics on given women or men and yet provide serviceable hypotheses for steering one's way through most social situations?

In the Gnostic case, the motherly divinity was associated with wisdom. Like Isis, the Gnostic goddesses focused on life and death. Certainly, the gods or male figures of divine power had a bearing on life and death, both physical and spiritual. But wisdom was more feminine than masculine. Wisdom was elliptic rather than direct, round rather than foursquare. One had to become subtle to outwit the forces imperiling one's salvation. The motherly Sophia could help one become subtle because she enjoyed a full measure of feminine subtlety, indirection, and awareness of all the tacit factors at work in psychological living and dying.

Beyond assumptions about men and women, about male and female characteristics, lie assumptions about the correlations or union between men and women. These latter assumptions concern more than directly physical intercourse. They bear on the fascinating yet maddening matter of what fuller consciousness may emerge from the interactions of men and women. For example, do mixed groups come to insights, levels of awareness, sensitivities, and emotional resonances measurably different from those of same-sex groups, either all female or all male?

Common sense and common report suggest that they do, but "measurably" is a hard criterion to meet. A priori, one can argue that simply by being together and having to interact, both men and women realize they are not the sum of humanity. Whenever the other sex is present, we cannot canonize our own kind, ways of doing things, or measures of wisdom. We may continue to disparage the other sex when it has departed, but in the presence of the other sex we are humbled and relativized. Certainly, some closed, dishonest men and women come away from heterosexual encounters confirmed in their prejudices. But honest men and women come away reminded that they ought to listen to the other voice, the one whose timbre they cannot produce in their own vocal cords.

Such honest people encounter a further obligation, of course, namely, to encourage such meetings of the sexes. Indeed, it is to go beyond the letter of "meeting" and seek the richest possible contribution of the other sex's point of view. More times than not nowadays, that will require both men's and women's working to get women's voices heard, women's points of view appreciated. To date, in our American culture, men control public space and time. Regularly, fine ideas that women might voice in private or among small groups of friends are lost because women do not have the courage and don't feel welcomed to speak up.

The more that one contemplates the assemblies in which important decisions emerge, the more important the fair representation of both sexes' experience becomes. Whether church assemblies discussing the ordination of practicing homosexuals and lesbians, state legislatures discussing funding for education, or local groups discussing the place of the arts in mainstream culture, the imperative is the same. We ought to draw on the fullest possible fund of communal wisdom. We cripple ourselves when we exclude or fail to welcome any distinctive group.

The first breakdown of human beings occurs along sexual lines. Without minimizing the significance of racial, economic, ethnic, or religious differences and so possible complementarities, supplements, and checks and balances, I believe that sexual distinctions are the first we have to honor if we wish adequate representation. But when we do honor sexual distinctions, we move toward the androgynous Gnostic deity. We say that a motherly wisdom is as important to our decisions as a fatherly power. We say that the end product of our deliberations, what we would see as our goal, if we were fully mature, is a whole humanity balancing female and male traits harmoniously. And we know, instinctively, that that sort of gnosis is neither esoteric nor heretical—it is orthodox to the bone.

LILITH

In rabbinic Judaism we meet a formidable female demon named Lilith. Gershom Scholem has unraveled the several different strands of tradition surrounding her. In the midrashic work (i.e., commentary) known as the *Alphabet of Ben Sira*, Lilith

> is identified with the "first Eve," who was created from the earth at the same time as Adam, and who, unwilling to forego her equality, disputed with him the manner of their intercourse. Pronouncing the Ineffable Name, she flew off into the air. On Adam's request, the Almighty sent after her the three angels Snwy, Snsnwy, and Smnglf; finding her in the Red Sea, the angels threatened that if she did not return, 100 of her sons would die every day. She refused, claiming that she was expressly created to harm newborn infants. However, she had to swear that whenever she saw the image of those angels in an amulet, she would lose her power over the infant. Here the legend concerning the wife of Adam who preceded the creation of Eve (Gen. 2) merges with the earlier legend of Lilith as a demon who kills infants and endangers women in childbirth.[7]

The cultural context is a Judaism alive with demons, amulets, and other picturesque ways of blending biblical images with folk traditions. Perhaps because they had already been subjected to numerous assaults by Gentiles, the Jews of the medieval period were highly suspectible to vivid depictions of evil powers. A full demonology flourished, along with an equally full repertoire of ways to ward off demonic assaults. The Lilith of Jewish folklore was not only the deviant first wife of Adam and the slayer of infants; she was also a wicked succubus who could corrupt the dreams of men, drawing them into illicit sexuality.

What are we to make of this bizarre, fascinating window into the psyche of not only medieval Judaism but also humanity's age-old association of women with witchcraft, demonology, and social deviance in general? Perhaps we should use it to remind us how frightening many patriarchal cultures have found any suggestion that women and femininity should be the equals of men and masculinity. We could remind ourselves that the androgyny intuited by the Gnostics, who speculated about the divinity necessary to redeem the fallen world, could strike terror in the hearts of people staking their lives on patriarchal cultural patterns.

There is no biblical tradition about Lilith. She stems from idle, or perhaps busily curious, speculation about what Adam did before God came to rescue him from his loneliness by creating him a "helpmeet" who would be flesh of his flesh and bone of his bone, the sum of his delight and desire. Before the disobedience of Adam and Eve, in the time when we might have expected perfect harmony, Jewish folk wisdom intuited a primordial trouble. Decoded, this intuition said that there was no idyllic time when disorder, rebellion against both God and human nature, was not possible. As soon as there was the human nature that we now know, with its sexual differentiation, there was the problem of coordination. From the first instant of sexual dimorphism, men and women had to negotiate, accommodate to their differences.

Lilith was the prototypical feminist in that she refused to subordinate herself to Adam. She would not bow to him, serve him, be the second sex. This was symbolized by her refusal to lie under him for sexual intercourse. She wanted to be on top, at least half the time. Being under Adam could have meant letting him rule her whole existence, determine her entire self. This she fought, from a deep instinct that it would be her ruin. Perhaps she already knew the restrictions on her independence that childbearing and childrearing would entail. Perhaps she already saw something imperial in Adam's bearing, some *libido dominandi*. Whatever the reason, Lilith in effect said to Adam the words associated with Lucifer, when he rebelled against God: "I will not serve."

For rabbinic Judaism, which was thoroughly patriarchal, this was an abomination. Implicit in Jewish patriarchy, as in that of Islam, Christianity, and all other species of men's claim to be the first and dominant sex, ran the fateful equation: women are to men as men are to God. Just as men ought to obey God in all things, so women ought to obey men in all things. The two relationships are symmetrical. The natural order of things is for

God to command men and for men to command women. Any violation of this natural order is idolatrous and ruinous.

The later association of Lilith, the first wife of Adam, with the demoness responsible for the deaths of infants was a gratuitous slur, but one psychologically coherent. It made perfect sense, in the nether world of the psyche, to attribute so unnatural an event as the death of an infant to the most unnatural of females, the rebellious first wife of Adam. She who ought to have been the mother of all living things would naturally hate the birth of any living descendant of Adam. Naturally, Eve would be her antagonist, for Lilith was bound to regret her fall from primeval power, the loss of her original status as the first of females. In seeking the lives of the newborn, she was venting her frustration, her howling sense of loss. Just as Lucifer became the avowed enemy of the children of Adam, who gained the intimacy with God that he had forfeited by his disobedience, so Lilith became the avowed enemy of women and children, those who most reminded her of what she had lost. The demonizing of Lilith, the prototypically disobedient woman, ran in the tracks of the demonizing of Lucifer, the Light-Bearer who became the Prince of Darkness.

A final note is that Lilith continued to be associated with sexuality. This fits an established patriarchal pattern. Again and again, we find that disobedient, threatening, deviant females are thought to destroy males by luring them into illict sex. Clearly, this is a projection of male fears of female allure, female sensual attraction. In this touching, almost funny mythologem, Lilith sets off all the alarms by wanting to be on top, to run the sexual operation. If women were to control sexual relations, anything might happen. Male desire, already so difficult to control, might break out in a dozen fearsome directions. Sexed into submission, men might never regain their dominant position, and without their dominant position, they would not know who they were. Faced with the prospect of a dominant other sex, or even a simply equal other sex, they could well crack up, fall into psychic crisis.

The relevance of this fear to present-day sexual pathologies such as rape and other abuses of women should be clear. Women can upset men simply by being. They do not necessarily have to do anything to cross men. They can simply be jogging through the park or walking home from work or cleaning the house. They can be toddlers or great-grandmothers, innocent or corrupt. Often it does not matter what sort of character they have developed. The mere fact of their sex triggers such anxieties or hatreds in men that men lash out blindly. Lilith is only one of the dozens of symbolic, mythical expressions of what men fear in women. Parallel to the psychopathology of much racism, we find that much sexual violence roots in deep-seated fears. Unstable men see women as proof that men's ways are not the only ways possible. They see the simple possibility that women will not agree with them or will oppose them as too much to bear. So in their sickness, such violent men try to do away with what opposes them. Rape is a crime of violence and degradation, not just of sexual desire. It is an effort to subordinate, force into submission, the other who proves that the world is richer, more complex, and so more threatening than what disturbed male egos can tolerate. Those egos are in rebellion against God because they cannot control God—cannot make the maker of the world place the world at their service. As the tinder sparking such rebellion, women can be hated doubly. Not only do they remind disturbed men that maleness is not the sum of humanity, they also remind them that in abusing women, they are rejecting God—sinning against God's order of creation. It is ironic, then, that Lilith and other uppity females should be castigated for unnatural acts. The most unnatural act possible between the sexes is hating the other form of humanity that God has made.

THE SHEKHINAH

In Jewish thought generally, the Shekhinah is the numinous presence of the divine in the world. However, in the esoteric schools of Jewish mysticism known as the Kabbalah, it becomes the feminine principle in the divine world, the world of the different *Sefirot*—numbers, or emanations of God. Moreover, the Shekhinah comes to summarize the divine world in relation to the world of creatures and to figure in the processes of redemption. As one authority puts it:

> All the elements and characteristics of the other *Sefirot* are represented within the *Shekhinah*. Like the moon, she has no light of her own, but receives the divine light from the other *Sefirot*. The main goal of the realm of the *Sefirot* (and of religious life as a whole) is to restore the true unity of God, the union of the masculine principle . . . and the *Shekhinah*, which was originally constant and undisturbed but was broken by the sins of Israel, by the machinations of the evil power . . . and by the exile. The restoration of the original harmony can be effected by the religious acts of the people of Israel through adhering to the Torah, keeping the commandments, and prayer.[8]

The Shekhinah is a major symbolism in the Kabbalah, coming to focus much of the mystics' desire. She is the sphere of divine power closest to the world. The created world owes its light to her, and its power. The angels serve the Shekhinah, as she mediates God's favors to Israel, and how Israel behaves shapes what she can be for it. Thus the battleground between good and evil passes through her. She becomes the hope of Jewish piety: "Study of the Torah and prayer bring a Jew near the *Shekhinah*, for she is symbolized as the Oral Law. The *Shekhinah* is the divine power usually revealed to the prophets, though sometimes higher divine powers may take part in such a revelation. She is also the first goal of the mystic."[9]

Here, then, we have a mystical version of many of the recurrent motifs in the mythology of feminine divinity. The emanations of God—God's inner movements, including those that bring divinity to the created world—have masculine and feminine characteristics. If one is to imagine the divine life (the proscriptions against constructing images of God could forbid such a project to Jews), one has to balance masculine attributes with feminine. Even so, from a divine point of view, the feminine attributes rank lower than the masculine. The Shekhinah is the lowest of the emanations, the one most distant from the inner core of divinity. If there is to be the perfect harmony that divinity requires, however, she must be reconciled with higher masculine spheres. By turns, this conviction led to the image of the Shekhinah as the bride of God. (The Sabbath could also be the bride of God.)

From a human point of view, though, the Shekhinah is more approachable than the higher Sefirot. She is the divine realm closest to the created world, so it is easy to think that she will be the most sympathetic. The pathetic need of the created world to repent of its sins and do good deeds to heal the ruptures caused by wayward Israel and Satan rises to the attention of the Shekhinah. This suggests that she is sympathetic to human beings' plight. Indeed, in some Kabbalistic schools, such as that of Isaac Luria, the Shekhinah herself is in exile because of Israel's sins. But mystical prayer can make contact with her and bring her back from exile to some degree. In advancing toward her, the mystic can verge upon union with the godhead. So she gains the allure of a beautiful face of the godhead. She becomes a valid symbol of what the pious soul can seek in love.

Some of the imagery of the Kabbalah is reminiscent of Gnosticism, with its falls and spheres. The process of redemption is depicted as mounting back to positions that once were held but then became lost. The glow of the godhead lights the way for those trying to return. Somewhat like Sophia, the Shekhinah is more approachable than the pure divine power, as a gentle mother is more approachable than a stern father. The Jewish stereotypes of the sexes were rich and complex, but on the whole women stood for the heart, while men stood for the head. Men studied while women ran the home, even the business. Men tried to rise above wayward passion, to live by reason and devotion to Torah. Women walked the way of love and good deeds, of self-sacrifice and devotion to husband and children. Thus to give the Shekhinah a feminine persona was to make it understanding and inviting.

What should present-day women make of this stereotype? How should they regard being considered the inviting sex, the approachable sex, the part of the imagery of God least likely to frighten little children, most likely to trade in smiles, warmth, and positive emotions? Complicated questions. First, there is no universal answer. Individual women have to decide for themselves how much of this stereotype feels comfortable—how much they want to affirm and try to enflesh. Second, it is hard to go against the grain. If the prevailing expectation is that the goodness of women models the truly kinder, gentler society that we hope to find with God, then women oppose that expectation at their peril. Indeed, they risk being labeled ungodly as well as surprising, disturbing, hard, and disappointing.

Third, it is possible to criticize the saccharine flavoring that the imagery can acquire, reminding oneself and others that the Shekhinah, and all other reflections of the femininity of God, need not be sweet and tamed. The Shekhinah is the luminous presence of God, the shining numinosity of God. One could argue that, fully appreciated, it becomes a blazing light against which one has to shield one's soul. Only when patriarchal theology domesticates the feminine, making the woman "little," does a feminine face for divinity become completely assuring, something one can surely gaze upon without fright. In itself, divinity is bound to frighten us, even though fright is not its final impact. "The beginning of wisdom is fear of the Lord"—and of the Lady as well. The end of wisdom, presumably, is love of the Lord—and of the Lady as well.

In the case of the Lady, the fear may be that one will disgrace oneself before what is utterly gracious. The motif of Lady Wisdom the world over is that she is gracious. The Shekhinah shares in this archetype, though she is not limited to it. The exile of the Shekhinah, due to the sins of Israel, humanizes the horrors of sin. Sin is not simply impossible, foolish revolt—senseless effort to deny the godness of God. It is also personal offense, dealt out in such coin as forgetfulness, loss of trust, and ingratitude. In addition to the raw horror of having tried to oppose the power that made the world from nothingness and is all-holy, there is in sin the refined horror of having been so self-absorbed that one became ungrateful and forgot one's greatest benefactor. Here the imagery of the human being as prodigal child seems inevitable, but the Shekhinah suggests that prodigal children sin against mothers as well as fathers. Mothers, the sources of life, sometimes receive for their services only ingratitude, neglect, and forgetfulness. One of the messages of the Shekhinah is that when we turn away from God and become unmindful of God's blessings, we deserve the punishments of exile. We have rejected our motherland, so we are bound to feel like people without a country.

Women may be tempted to identify themselves with the Shekhinah and so focus on all the forgetfulness and ingratitude visited upon them by their children, spouses, and friends. We have to be sure that we also consider how we ourselves forget our benefactors, show ourselves to have no memories or gratitude. Above all, religious women have to consider how they have been ungrateful to God. If it helps them to picture God as a bountiful female, the best of mothers, let such pictures abound. Under whatever imagery, though, the examination of one's sins of ingratitude is salutary.

Such an examination should not be a soul scraping that further lowers one's perhaps already low self-esteem. It should rather be a contemplation that raises our estimate of God, who wants only our return to mental health, our recall of how things actually stand between us and our Creator.

And how do things actually stand between us and our Creator? Jewish theology has to say: astoundingly well. The Creator has looked upon creation, ourselves included, and called it very good. The Creator has initiated covenants, marriages, myriad ties that bind. If we will, we can find the Creator in our midst, sojourning with us, sharing our journey. Certainly, God will be with us as God chooses. Certainly the Shekhinah approaches and recedes, glows or turns cold, in function of the mysteries of grace and sin, and so not as something we can manipulate. Still, there would be no Skekhinah-for-us, no cloud by day and pillar of fire by night, if God had not determined to be gracious unconditionally, to love us unconditionally. The sins of Israel have never been the whole story. In the Davidic theology, the Lord's covenant is irrevocable. In the marrow of our peoplehood, we have a pledge that God will never repent of having made us. In our dark nights, that pledge can be a lifeline.

People who suffer clinical depressions find it nearly impossible to believe that anyone could pledge to stand by them, no matter what. Now and then, though, when the clouds open, they can find their hope renewed, as they see that spouse, friend, or God has stood by. All of us are liable to depression when we consider the darkness of history and the darkness of our own hearts. Still, we may read the myths and symbols of the past hopefully.

For example, through the biblical symbols and the images of the Kabbalah, many pious Jews have slogged through daunting suffering. In their own way, with their own accents, they have said, "The Lord has put forth a gracious countenance in the past. Perhaps he will do so again. The movements of our God closest to our wretched created sphere have appeared lovely and welcoming, in the Shekhinah. When we surrender to her charm, or at least try not to despair that one day we shall again find her charming, we do God great credit. For we say that not even exile can keep us from holding God to her promises. Not even our own sins can take away her sovereign beauty. Verily, the Shekhinah bears us the glowing presence of God, when and as God wishes. Verily, our task is to pay attention, keep a lookout, spy for her smile and welcome. If we do, we cannot fail to find her. For our God is compassionate and merciful, longsuffering, slow to anger and abiding in steadfast love. Our God is our queen and mother. Could she ever let us down?"

JESUS

In chapters 59 and 60 of the long version of *Showings*, by the late medieval English Christian mystic Julian of Norwich (1342–

after 1416), we find a remarkable imagery. There Jesus appears as the mother of the spiritual lives of those who cling to him by faith. The long version of Julian's text is the fruit of many years' deliberation. It took her several decades to realize the full implications of the experiences granted her in young adulthood, when she was on the verge of death. So this imagery of the motherhood of Jesus stands at the center of her mature faith. Let us first attend to her own words (as translated into modern English) and then reflect on their significance in the context of our study of mythology about women.

From this it follows that as truly as God is our Father, so truly is God our Mother. Our Father wills, our Mother works, and our good Lord the Holy Spirit confirms. And therefore it is our part to love our God in whom we have our being, reverently thanking and praising him for our creation, mightily praying to our Mother for mercy and pity, and to our Lord the Holy Spirit for help and grace. . . . And so Jesus is our true Mother in nature by our first creation, and he is our true Mother in grace by his taking our created nature. All the lovely works and all the sweet loving offices of beloved motherhood are appropriated to the second person, for in him we have this godly will, whole and safe forever, both in nature and in grace, from his own goodness proper to him. . . . Our mother in nature, our Mother in grace, because he wanted altogether to become our Mother in all things, made the foundation of his work most humbly and most mildly in the maiden's womb . . . himself to do the service and the office of motherhood in everything. The mother's service is nearest, readiest, and surest: nearest because it is most natural, readiest because it is most loving, and surest because it is truest. No one ever might or could perform this office fully, except only him . . . our true Mother Jesus, he alone bears us for joy and for endless life, blessed may he be. So he carries us within him in love and travail, until the full time when he wanted to suffer the sharpest thorns and cruel pains that ever were or will be, and at the last he died. . . . He could not die any more, but he did not want to cease working; therefore he must needs nourish us, for the precious love of motherhood has made him our debtor. The mother can give her child to suck of her milk, but our precious Mother

Jesus can feed us with himself, and does, most courteously and most tenderly, with the blessed sacrament, which is the precious food of true life. . . . The mother can lay her child tenderly to her breast, but our tender Mother Jesus can lead us easily into his blessed breast through his sweet open side, and show us there a part of the godhead and of the joys of heaven with inner certainty of endless bliss. . . . This fair lovely word "mother" is so sweet and so kind in itself that it cannot truly be said of anyone or to anyone except of him, and to him who is the true Mother of life and of all things . . . and in this I saw that every debt which we owe by God's command to fatherhood and motherhood is fulfilled in truly loving God, which blessed love Christ works in us. And this was revealed in everything, and especially in the great bounteous words [of a prior revelation] when he says: I am he whom you love.[10]

First, it is as fitting to predicate motherhood of God as fatherhood. Despite the centrality of masculine—indeed patriarchal—language in the Bible, Christians can speak of God as their Mother. Certainly, Jesus called God his Father. Certainly, the central Christian prayer is the "Our Father." But Julian's own experience assures her that God is also feminine. The love that mothers bear their children is an intimate, crucial analogy for the love and nature of God. When she parses this experience in terms of the Christian understanding of God as a Trinity of divine "persons," Julian attributes motherhood particularly to the second person—the Son, or Word—who took flesh from the Virgin Mary and became Jesus of Nazareth. If the Father is the ultimate source of creation and salvation, Jesus the Son is the one who works out the Father's will. This work, being so fully a matter of love and nurture, is like nothing so much as a motherhood.

Second, for Julian we glimpse the full significance of maternal love only when we make Jesus the prime analogate. Indeed, it is from the love he bears humankind that we get our fullest sense of what begetting life and nourishing it import. The deepest reaches of human begetting, nourishment, and life are those where God makes the human being an image and likeness of the divine being. This making is a gestation and feeding best appropriated (assigned) to the Son. So Julian imagines the Son as bearing forth children of grace (divine life) in travail. She assimilates the sufferings of Jesus on the cross to his carrying children for God and giving them birth painfully. At his death, he had not exhausted his love or sense of responsibility for his beloved children. So he arranged to become their nourishment, much as a mother nourishes her children from her own body. The eucharistic sacrament, in which Christians believe they receive the substance of Christ, his body and blood, is like the nursing of God's children.

Similarly, the way that Jesus takes to himself those who seek him in prayer and assures them that all will be well, in heaven, is reminiscent of a mother comforting a child at her breast. The medieval tradition of contemplating the scenes of the New Testament as living icons of God's being and ways allows Julian to fix on the pierced side of Christ as a feminine figure. John 19:33–34 is the text Julian has in mind. After Jesus has died on the cross, the soldiers come to take him down: "But when they came to Jesus and saw that he was already dead, they did not break his legs. Instead, one of the soldiers pierced his side with a spear, and at once blood and water came out." Christian symbolists have long regarded this blood and water as a reference to the sacraments of the Eucharist and baptism. Julian is saying that the maternal breast of Jesus gives Christians all they need for eternal life. The reference to opening a vision of part of the godhead and the joys of heaven is a further development, not found in the Gospel of John, but part of Julian's vision of Christ. It suggests that in taking the faithful to his bosom, Christ the Mother comforts them with a preview of heavenly bliss.

What are we to make of this elaboration of the loving offices of Christ in terms of a divine motherhood? First, that it was not a tendency unique to Julian of Norwich. For example, Carolyn Walker Bynum, among others, has studied texts from the twelfth and thirteenth centuries, many of them written by Cistercians shaped by Bernard of Clairvaux, in which Jesus appears as the mother of divine life in Christians.[11] Second, that it represents a triumph of common sense. The patriarchal tendency to arrogate symbols of authority to masculinity has always been thwarted by the brute biological fact that females are as essential to procreation and culture as males.

We have seen the appearance of many female deities in the pantheons of Eastern and Near Eastern peoples. The exclusion of female symbols for the divine in mainstream Christian theology bucks a worldwide trend. Only by imposing an impossible psychology have Christian theologians been able to suggest that divinity is either purely male or at least more male than female. In fact, the high Christian theological tradition has always taught that God is beyond sex, in the sense that none of the limitations implied in sexuality can apply to the divinity. God cannot be male, if that suggests the exclusion of female attributes or virtues in God. God cannot be "Father" in a way that denies tenderness, nourishment, fertility, beauty, or any of the other stereotypically feminine positive qualities. But Christians have not been taught to pray to God as their mother, while they have been taught, on the model of Jesus, to pray to God as their father. Many of their prayers to the Virgin Mary have sought to fill this lacuna, but those prayers cannot target divinity as such, on pain of being idolatrous. Only God deserves worship, in the strict sense, and for orthodox Christian faith the Virgin Mary is not God. So in addressing Jesus as motherly, Julian and others were breaking through strong but psychologically unsupportable barriers. They were creating ways to give people access to some of their warmest analogies for the divine love.

It is no suprise that Julian's theology, overall, is more positive than what we find in many other Christian writers, both before her historical period and after it. Her view of the motherhood of Jesus is part and parcel of a vision in which one cannot exaggerate the goodness of God. The twin virtues that the person traveling Julian's spiritual path needs to complete the journey are patience and hope. The great vices or obstacles are impatience and despair. The problem is not the goodness of God but the tendency of human sinfulness to block faith in this goodness and so make it hard for people to interpret what God metes out to them as effects of the divine love. Even with the most powerful imagery one could think of—the divine taking flesh and dying for human beings to change their miserable situation—people keep forgetting, disbelieving, the divine goodness. Julian would have such people think of Jesus' various works on their behalf according to the analogy of the best human love that she knows: the self-sacrificing devotion of mothers, who give their children flesh from their own flesh, food from their own breasts, tender concern throughout all their lives.

Naturally, one has to enter the caveat that pinning one's depictions of the divine on the analogy of human parenthood has great pitfalls. If people have abusive parents, mothers or fathers, they are going to recoil from picturing God as a loving mother or father. Still, almost all of us know, either positively or by default, the importance of parental love. Almost all of us can take comfort from the message that Julian proclaims. Her God is infinitely tender, caring, and loving. Like the prophet Isaiah, she can no more imagine God abandoning his people than she can imagine a nursing mother abandoning her child. We know, unfortunately, that on occasion nursing mothers do abandon their children—when, for instance, they are on drugs or feel they can no longer go on. But this merely raises sobering questions about the social factors and the abuses of personal freedom that produce such perversions of feminine humanity. On the whole, the imagery that Julian received in her visions is a wonderful demonstration of the full share that women can feel they have in the best, the most ultimate, of realities: that of a fully loving God.

THE VIRGIN MARY

In discussing the motherhood of Jesus, we entered into Christian feminine mythology. Jesus could be a mother only by analogy, through a symbolic reading of his nurturing love. Any stories of his bringing Christian faith to birth and nourishing had to be mythological, in the sense of conveying a drama and truth that fall outside space and time. They occur in history, but not through appearances that historians normally recognize. Like the Christian accounts of the operation of the eucharistic elements of bread and wine, they require faith for acceptance.

Much the same holds for the Christian interpretations of the career and significance of the Virgin Mary. The only original information we have about Mary of Nazareth, the mother of Jesus, comes from the New Testament, where her experience and significance are much shaped by faith that Jesus the Christ, the crucified and risen head of the Christian community, has brought definitive salvation. It is interesting that the most prominent imagery about the Virgin Mary occurs at the beginning and end of Jesus's life. It is also interesting that the modern dogmatic declarations about Mary stress the beginning and end of her own life.

At the beginning of Jesus' life, Mary conceives him supernaturally, through the agency of the Holy Spirit, the third person of the Christian Trinity. The New Testament reports this experience as a triumph of innocence and fidelity, worked according to God's providential design:

In the sixth month [of the pregnancy of Mary's relative Elizabeth, the mother of John the Baptist] the angel Gabriel was sent by God to a town in Galilee called Nazareth, to a virgin engaged to a man whose name was Joseph, of the house of David. The Virgin's name was Mary. And he came to her and said, "Greetings, favored one! The Lord is with you." But she was much perplexed by his words and pondered what sort of greeting this might be. The angel said to her, "Do not be afraid, Mary, for you have found favor with God. And now, you will conceive in your womb and bear a son, and you will name him Jesus. He will be great, and will be called the Son of the Most High, and the Lord God will give to him the throne of his ancestor David. He will reign over the house of Jacob forever, and of his kingdom there will be no end." Mary said to the angel, "How can this be, since I am a virgin?" The angel said to her, "The Holy Spirit will come upon you, and will overshadow you; therefore the child to be born will be holy; he will be called Son of God. And now, your relative Elizabeth in her old age has also conceived a son; and this is the sixth month for her who was said to be barren. For nothing will be impossible with God." Then Mary said, "Here am I, the servant of the Lord; let it be with me according to your word." Then the angel departed from her. (Luke 1:26–38)

At the end of Jesus' life, when he hung dying on the cross, Mary stood by, faithful and desolate. This scene engraved itself in Christian imagination, contributing to her designation Sorrowful Mother. The scene of her conception of Jesus, usually known as the Annunciation, rivaled the scene of her giving birth to Jesus in a manger in Bethlehem. In fact, Christian artists delighted in the full imagery of the Madonna, from the virginal conception of her child to his birth and death. Mary and Jesus became not only archetypes of mother and child but signs of the complete entry of the Christian divinity into history—human affairs and human flesh. Theologians praised Mary as the *theotokos*, the bearer of God, considering her flesh the anchor of the Incarnation (the Christian conviction that the Word of God took flesh and became fully human).

What greater intimacy could there have been, than for divinity to make itself one with humanity, truly become like human beings in all things except sin? And what imagery better expressed this central Christian conviction than that of the birth of Jesus, celebrated each year at Christmas? The holy conception of Jesus by Mary, her willingness to become the mother of God, became the paradigm of faithful Christian living. Just as she had said, "Here I am, the servant of the Lord," so all faithful Christians would say. Mary's fidelity continued throughout Jesus's life, and it did not flag at his death—that was the bedrock conviction of the Christian faithful who sought her help.

Traditional Christians often prayed to the Sorrowful Mother, thinking of her as the Madonna who had had to undergo the unnatural experience of receiving into her arms the dead body of her son, the child she had once held to nurse. Michelangelo's *Pietà*, enshrined in the central church of Catholic Christendom, St. Peter's in Rome, expressed the profound impact of this Marian mythology. The pathos of Jesus' sufferings on the cross received a final punctuation in the reception of his dead body by his mother. There the sorrowful mystery reached its nadir. There the apparently universal vocation of women to mourn for the dead, lament the laceration of the flesh they have created, came to unparalled expression.

Because of her constant fidelity and of her having anchored the economy of salvation, Mary the Mother of God was a powerful intercessor before God. Christians immersed in the mythology of her relationship to Jesus could believe that Jesus would refuse her nothing. Anything that she asked he would grant most willingly, for if she was the most faithful mother, he had to be the most dutiful son. Divine though he was, he had to be fully pleased with her who had served the will of his Father so perfectly. Thus in popular medieval imagination Mary became the Queen of Heaven. Those who went to her in petition could be assured of a favorable reception from Christ, and a favorable reception from Christ meant a favorable reception from the Father, who was completely one with Christ. Consequently Mary stood apart from the rest of the saints, on a plateau all her own. Less than divine but more than all other mortals, she made feminine grace a wonderful adornment of heaven.

The desire to elaborate the glories of Mary had much to do with the development of two articles of Catholic faith defined on her behalf in the nineteenth and twentieth centuries. When they contemplated the beginnings of Mary's own life, devout Marianists reasoned that she could never have sinned. If she were to bear worthily a child who was truly and fully divine, God from God and light from light, as the creed affirmed, Mary must have been free of the taint of original sin. Original sin, a notion derived from the account of the disobedience of Adam and Eve in Genesis, kept human beings from intimacy with

God. But Mary was accorded the greatest intimacy with God conceivable. The angel told her that she had found such favor with God that she was to bear the Son of God. Meditating on this imagery, Marian theologians developed the notion of Mary's "immaculate conception." From the beginning of her own existence, in the womb of her own mother, Mary must have been free of original sin. That was the only congruous, fitting way to think about her state of soul.

Relatedly, at the end of her life, Mary must have escaped the implications, the penalties, of original sin. Though there are no scriptural references to the death of Mary, pious theologians reasoned that she must have been "assumed" into heaven without bodily disintegration. Unlike the death of ordinary, sinful human beings, which entailed the separation of the body from the spirit, Mary must have been taken into heaven bodily. There, with Jesus, she would enjoy the bliss of heaven as an integral human person, a fully material being. All other human beings would have to wait for a "general" resurrection and judgment before receiving their heavenly bodies. As the sinless mother of God, however, Mary had not had to wait. So, her queenship of heaven could be imagined as a continuance of the beautiful motherhood she had exercised on earth. She must be not a disembodied spirit, however holy, but a fully living being of flesh and blood, exulting in the triumph of her Son and his reign with the Father and Spirit in endless fulfillment.

At the conclusion of her thorough but somewhat skeptical study of the mythology of the Virgin Mary, Marina Warner summarizes the archetypal status that Marian imagery attained in Western history.

Nothing it seems, even to non-Catholics, could be more natural than this icon of feminine perfection, built on the equivalence between goodness, motherhood, purity, gentleness, and submission. To take a random, visual example: in the beautiful school of Giotto panel now at Oxford . . . the Virgin is serene, sagacious, exquisitely fulfilled as the Christ child on her arm reaches up and touches her cheek with his tiny hand and clutches at the neckline of her dress. She tenderly hovers with delicate tapering fingers to catch him if he struggles too vigorously. Her eyes, as in so much Marian iconography, gaze out beyond the picture frame to dwell on an inner landscape of the soul, where tragedy and triumph are bound together, and her countenance is therefore wistful. Wistfulness seems also a natural quality of the feminine, a part of modesty and grace, a suitable expression of wonderment at her own beauty and mystery, a kind of hesitancy and humility that is hardly ever present in images of masculine beauty and goodness. In such an icon as this school of Giotto painting—the beauty of which no one would deny, just as I am not saying that motherhood, purity, gentleness are evil or ugly in themselves—the interlocking of myth and ideology is camouflaged. Without any duplicity or malevolence on the painter's part, myriad assumptions are limpidly and luminously made. Assumptions about role satisfaction, sexual differences, beauty, and goodness are all wondrously compressed in this one icon, just as they are in every artefact produced by the cult of the Virgin Mary.[12]

It would be fascinating to study the cultural permutations of Marian mythology, for example, by examining the different cultuses displayed at various Marian shrines (Lourdes, Guadelupe, and the many others). Again and again we find Christians, ancient and contemporary, recurring to the Virgin—for help with physical troubles, to define their cultural identity, to ward off the specters of godless Communism. Mary has been not only the archetype of a certain feminine beauty and goodness but also the victor over sorest suffering—the mother whose heart was broken by the murder of her son but who yet endured.

Pious Christian speculation often suggested that, before appearing to his disciples, the risen Christ must have appeared to his mother. It would have been only fitting. In dozens of other ways, popular, folk Christianity often made the work of Jesus a partnership with his mother. In so doing, it expanded the central Christian story of salvation so that it became a male-female collaboration. Thus the three quasi-male figures of the Trinity were not the only actors in the drama of salvation. Of great importance also was a wondrous heroine, the Virgin Mother, who had joined her sufferings to those of the suffering Christ and so could understand all the pains of the audience—the simple folk desperate for her help.

MARY IN THE QUR'AN

For the Qur'an, Mary is both the mother of a great prophet, Jesus, and a fine muslim (submitter to God) in her own right. The daughter of Imran and Hannah, she was raised by Zachariah. Her mother dedicated her to the Lord, who received her as a holy offering and put her in the care of the priest Zachariah. She grew up comely and frequented the sanctuary, where people prayed to God. "Whenever Zachariah went in to her in the Sanctuary, he found her provisioned. 'Mary,' he said, 'how comes this to thee?' 'From God,' she said. Truly God provisions whosoever He will without reckoning" (3:33).[13] Not only was Mary the object of God's special care, she became an example of pious love of the mosque. Indeed, Muslim tradition associated her with the mihrab, the especially holy niche in the mosque pointing in the direction of Mecca. Thus verse 3:33 often adorns the mihrab, as though to remind visitors to follow Mary's example.

Chapter 19 of the Qur'an, traditionally entitled "Mary," explains her conception and delivery of Jesus.

And you shall recount in the Book the story of Mary: how she left her people and betook herself to a solitary place to the east. We sent to her Our spirit in the semblance of a full-grown man. And when she saw him she said: "May the Merciful defend me from you! If you fear the Lord, leave me and go your way." "I am the messenger of your Lord," he replied, "and have come to give you a holy son." "How shall I bear a child," she answered, "when I am a virgin, untouched by man?" "Such is the will of your

Lord," he replied. "That is no difficult thing for him. 'He shall be a sign to mankind,' says the Lord, 'and a blessing from Our self. That is Our decree.'"

Thereupon she conceived, and retired to a far-off place. And when she felt the throes of childbirth she lay down by the trunk of a palm-tree, crying: "Oh, would that I had died and passed into oblivion!" But a voice from below cried out to her: "Do not despair. Your Lord has provided a brook that runs at your feet, and if you shake the trunk of this palm-tree it will drop fresh ripe dates in your lap. Therefore rejoice. Eat and drink, and should you meet any mortal say to him: 'I have vowed a fast to the Merciful and will not speak with any man today.'" Then she took the child to her people, who said to her: "This is indeed a strange thing! Sister of Aaron, your father was never a whore-monger, nor was your mother a harlot." She made a sign to them, pointing to the child. But they replied: "How can we speak with a babe in the cradle?"

Whereupon he spoke and said: "I am the servant of Allah. He has given me the Gospel and ordained me a prophet. His blessing is upon me wherever I go, and He has commanded me to be steadfast in prayer and to give alms to the poor as long as I shall live. He has exhorted me to honour my mother and has purged me of vanity and wickedness. I was blessed on the day I was born, and blessed I shall be on the day of my death; and may peace be upon me on the day when I shall be raised to life." Such was Jesus, the son of Mary. That is the whole truth, which they are unwilling to accept. Allah forbid that He Himself should beget a Son! When He decrees a thing He need only say: "Be," and it is. (19:16–34)[14]

Much is going on in this text. Muslims generally believe that Muhammad received the Qur'an directly from Allah. They therefore discount any influence from Jewish or Christian sources. When a biblical tradition, a story narrated in the Old or New Testament, occurs in a new form in the Qur'an, the Muslim view is that the version in the Qur'an is the true account, while the other versions are misguided.

Here we have a tradition, not found in the New Testament, about the travail of Mary. She receives the "annunciation" from a messenger in solitude. When she first sees him, she fears, like a virtuous and vulnerable girl. She cannot understand his promise that she will conceive a holy son, because she knows she is a virgin. A virgin birth is no difficulty for Allah, however. If he has decided to raise up a man who will be a sign to humanity (of how they are to live), it will be accomplished. Jesus will be a blessing to humankind (with the implication that Mary is privileged to conceive him).

The account in the Qur'an does not mention Mary's agreement. When the holy spirit has finished his announcement, she conceives. Just as God provided for her in her youth, giving her food in the sanctuary, so he provides for her in the wilderness, at the time of her birth pangs. Miraculously, he sustains her with water and dates. The implication in the account of her bringing the child to her people is that she had to suffer their suspicions that the child was illegitimate. The infant's miraculous speaking vindicates her. He is a servant of Allah, who has given him the gospel (which means that the gospel is part of divine providence—valuable, even though superseded by the Qur'an). The child Jesus will be a prophet. His life will be marked by prayer and almsgiving. (Almsgiving does not characterize the Jesus of the New Testament, but it is a requisite for a pious Muslim.)

In saying that Allah has purged him of vanity and wickedness, the child (and the Qur'an) lays the foundation for a doctrine of Jesus' sinlessness. God blessed him when he was born, and God blessed him when he died. (The Qur'an denies that Jesus truly died on the cross. He merely appeared to die.) There is nothing more to the significance of Jesus. The Christian view that he was the Son of God is completely wrong. Allah has no need of a Son. Placing anything created alongside Allah is a blasphemy.

The Muslim mythology of Mary and Jesus therefore differs considerably from the Christian. Nonetheless, it honors both Mary and Jesus, placing them in the line of exemplary Muslims.

Jesus was a great prophet, calling his people to true worship of God. Mary enabled the prophetic work of Jesus to occur, and she herself showed great faith in Allah. As Aaron was to Moses, so was Mary to Jesus. She helped a great prophetic work, cooperating with it inwardly.

If we step apart from the Qur'an's own assumptions to reflect on the transposition of the Marian materials in their passage from their Christian origins to their Muslim rearrangment, we gain a valuable insight into the relationship that Islam wants to maintain with Christianity. Islam sees itself as the perfecting of Christianity, not its denial. Muhammad perfects the prophecy of Jesus, as of the Israelite prophets on whose work Jesus improved. Humanity is always in need of prophecy. Again and again, forgetful, weak people need to be called back to the fundamentals. However, the fundamentals boil down to faith in Allah, the one God, whom Muhammad has publicized perfectly. Thus there will be no improvement upon the Qur'an, no supercession by a later prophecy. Mary and Jesus are venerable and important, in the measure that they illustrate faith in the one God and help others to gain it.

Because they have not considered Jesus divine and so have not considered Mary to be the mother of God, Muslims have had no cult of a holy female intimately tied to divinity. They have had no art depicting the birth of the divine child, no sorrowful mother standing by the cross of the divine man. When they have prayed, no queen of heaven has adorned their imagination of the court of Allah. No shrines to Mary have dotted the landscape of Muslim countries.

The official Muslim theology has been that God should not be represented. It would lead the mind astray to depict God in any way. Allah stands so far beyond the human, created realm that depictions would only falsify people's faith. The crux of that faith is submission, the deeper and less questioning the better. God did not become human. No Son of God has taken flesh. So no Muslim saints have mimicked Julian of Norwich in speaking of God as a mother, of Christ as the soul's divine nurse. Similarly, no Muslim chapels have featured madonnas tenderly restraining divine children. As a result, Mary is not in Muslim mythology the archetypal female, representative of all things gentle and pure. The Qur'an praises her piety and her courage, but it does not make her the *theotokos*, the source of God's flesh.

It would be bold indeed to speculate on the ties between these differences in the Christian and Muslim conceptions of Mary and the treatment of women in the two cultural spheres, since both have abused women in diverse ways. But perhaps it is fair to say that Christian mythology has forced people to contend with a sacral femininity that has had no place in Islam. Certainly Islam has honored female saints. But Islam has not worshiped an incarnate deity, and so it has not been forced to ponder the implications of Mary's miraculous conception of Jesus as assiduously as Christianity has.

Muslims might pray to Mary, but she could in no way be for them the special intercessor that Christian prayer has often made her. Nor could she assure Muslim women of their centrality to salvation as she assured Christian women. Thus Mary has played a crucial role in the entirely different "feel" that the Christian and Muslim pieties have enjoyed. The more Christians have homed to the enfleshment of divinity in Jesus, the more they have thought about the Madonna and the complete intimacy of God with humankind. In contrast, if Mary was as the Qur'an portrayed her, God need not, should not be thought of as having delivered himself into human keeping. For the New Testament, God let Mary determine the course of salvation, showing her a trust that eventually rendered the difference between heaven and earth negligible. This is an amazing view of divinity, and Muslims are bound to find it unacceptable. Thus Mary is a crucial source of the divide separating Islam and Christianity. Without her possessing the status of the mother of God, Christianity would be much closer to Islam.

FATIMAH

An editorial in the *New York Times* of February 10, 1989, warned the Bush administration that in reconsidering relations with Iran, it would be foolish to forget the cruelty associated with the regime of the Ayatollah Khomeini. The central item in the editorial's argument was the following:

In January, according to the Iranian news agency, Ayatollah Khomeini was deeply offended by a radio interview in which a woman said she could not accept the prophet Muhammad's daughter as a role model. As a result, the broadcast director at the Teheran Radio, Mohammad Arab Mazar-Yazdi, was sentenced to five years in jail. Three directors of the Teheran Radio's islamic ideology group were sentenced to four years each. All received 50 lashes. The court levying these penalties held that the broadcast 'notoriously misportrayed the ruling mentality of Iranian women.' Had the insult been deliberate, said the Ayatollah, the person responsible would have been executed.[15]

The Prophet Muhammad's daughter in question is Fatimah, about whom *The Concise Encyclopedia of Islam* states:

One of the three daughters of the Prophet, whose mother was Khadijah, the Prophet's first wife. The Prophet commended Fatimah's character, calling her one of the four exemplary women that he extolled in history, and she is usually referred to as *Fatimah az-zahra* ("Fatimah the resplendent"). She married the Prophet's cousin Ali ibn Abi Talib, who became the fourth Caliph; and their sons Hasan and Husayn are the ancestors of the *sharifs*, the descendants of the Prophet. For the Shi'ites [many of whom are Iranians], certain descendants of Ali and Fatimah through the line of Husayn are Imams, in the special Shi'ite sense of the term, which is that of divinely empowered spiritual leaders. A third son of Ali and Fatimah, Muhsin, died in infancy. Fatimah died six months after the Prophet's death and is buried in the *al-Baqi* cemetery in Medina. A sepulchre called Fatimah's Tomb is located near the tomb of the Prophet in the Prophet's mosque. Some, notably Shi'ites, believe this sepulchre to hold her body, but that is unlikely, despite the name, and it is far more probable that the body is actually in the nearby *al-Baqi* cemetery. She is held in great reverence by the Sunnis as well as by the Shi'ites.[16]

What are we to make of the incident reported in the *New York Times*, against the background supplied by *The Concise Encyclopedia of Islam*? What grist does it offer our feminist mythological mill? First, the obvious reaction to the account of the Ayatollah Khomeini's actions (in response to the Iranian woman who said that she could not accept Fatimah as a role model) is incredulity and horror: the mildest criticism verges on being a capital offense? Second, the more studied reaction is likely to be wonder at the depth of the Ayatollah's anger, and so curiosity about what irrational triggers the woman's statement had pulled. Following this line of inquiry, one soon comes to the heart of much fundamentalist Muslim behavior nowadays: putatively holy rage at the infidel West, which Muslims believe has been assaulting the soul of Islam.

If one wants to understand the furor about the veiling of women, for example, one has to grasp the pivotal role that the seclusion of women has played in traditional Muslim psychology. For example, when young Palestinian men in Gaza threaten women not wearing the veil, they think they are defending Islam. That they are also exhibiting an egregious male chauvinism is beside the point. To their mind, the Qur'an places men in charge of women, and the purity of women is the key to the survival of Islam. Women are not the equals of men, and the survival of Islam is the foremost task incumbent on all Muslims. The syllogism is clear: Wearing the veil is essential to the survival of Islam. You are not wearing the veil. Therefore you are a threat to the survival of Islam. The further conclusion is: Therefore I have the right to force you back to righteous living, if need be by force, since I am obliged to ensure the survival of Islam.

The holes in this reasoning are so obvious that we can pass them by. The slightest intuition that men and women must be equal in the sight of God devastates the entire argument. But more important is the fierce emotion exhibited by both the Ayatollah Khomeini and the young men of Gaza. Clearly they have so forcefully identified with Islam their entire selves—their honor, their responsibility before God, everything that makes their lives significant—that what they think threatens Islam becomes a murderous assault on their own being. Whether they actually think they can speak for God, so that this assault merits holy counterwarfare (*jihad*), is dubious in the case of the youths of Gaza, but not so dubious in the case of the Ayatollah. He had no scruples about acting as a hanging judge. He was quite willing to send thousands to their deaths if that was necessary to keep Islam pure. God had put such weighty responsibility in his hands, and he was not loathe to bear it.

When one ruminates about the incident at Teheran Radio, it seems likely that Fatimah was not significant in herself, but her ties to the Prophet made her a linchpin of Shi'ite faith. Not to exalt her as a paragon and exemplar of Muslim femininity was to call into question the entire edifice of Islamic faith. If women did not comport themselves according to the traditions that Fatimah represented, Islam might well fall apart.

Perhaps this is the juncture at which to reflect on the dangers of religious mythology and spotlight the responsibility of scholars to enter critical caveats. At the outset, we should admit that Fatimah, like the Virgin Mary, has served women well. The honor traditionally accorded her assured Muslim women that obeying their fathers, supporting their husbands, and raising children (especially boys) was a straight path to the Garden of Heaven. Moreover, the sufferings that overtook her husband, Ali, and her sons cast a veil of martyrdom around Fatimah herself, even though she had died shortly after her father's death, before those sufferings. The Shi'ites have always indulged a piety full of laments for the martyrdom of their leaders, Hasan and Husayn in particular. They have always tied this lamentation to their status as the minority portion of Islam, lesser in numbers than the Sunnis, and their closer connections with the bloodline of the Prophet. So to cast any aspersions on the status of Fatimah could seem callous, unmindful of the high cost paid by her family. The contemporary Iranian woman doubting Fatimah could seem to be doubting the history by which the Ayatollah Khomeini, and many for whom he spoke, directed their lives.

How is it possible to defend so fierce a traditionalism? Only if one rejects the modern Western embrace of tolerance. In effect, those who agree with the passions that drove the Ayatollah Khomeini write modern Western history off as a great defection from God. Fundamentalist Islam, refusing to move much beyond the words of the Qur'an and the traditional interpretations of those words, cannot accept the notion that individuals have rights of conscience that no human agency should ride over. The woman voicing her opinion about Fatimah has no right to free speech. There is no need to honor her perceptions, her exegesis of her own conscience, because she clashes with holy tradition. Holy tradition is impregnable. Certainly, Islam has developed various ways of trying to update its cultural practices, but to be acceptable to the mainstream, any updatings have to ensure the primacy of Qur'anic revelation and the example of the Prophet. We do not know what the doubting Iranian woman thought would be a proper role model. Perhaps the interviewers never got to probe her ideas that deeply. We only know that she violated the principle, dear to fundamentalist Muslims, that established practice cannot be overthrown, cannot even be questioned directly.

So the myth ruling the reaction of the Ayatollah, and of the many who have supported him, is rich, complex, profound. The special offense in the case of the radio interview was that a woman should presume to question tradition, but the central issue went beyond anything feminist. What we might call a holy patriarchy rules in fundamentalist Islam. In the name of Allah, the male overseers of tradition believe they have to counter every threat to longstanding Qur'anic interpretation. The story ruling their souls is that they are the repositories of God's own truth, the powers designated to avenge offenses against the divine dignity. The fact that this is a story more likely rooted in their own psyches than in anything historical or critically defensible shows the hunger on which mythology depends. What space and time can never provide—surety of divine guidance, even of divine approval—comes forth from another venue.

From that venue, "faith" becomes not the rational submission of the finite human being to the infinite mystery of God but the passionate defense of historically conditioned traditions. This is a problem that all religions based on historical revelations face. Judaism and Christianity are as liable to fundamentalist interpretation as Islam. At the current historical juncture, though, it happens that Islam is the tradition feeling most threatened by the modern drift of history. Judaism and Christianity have made their accommodations to modernity, sometimes gracefully, sometimes awkwardly. The mainstream of those two traditions has accepted the sacredness of the individual conscience, at least to the extent of proscribing any death dealing to heretics. But the mainstream of Islam has yet to make this move, yet to agree to this reading of human conscience. The consequences are enormous, especially for women.

Without the right to determine their own identity, Muslim women become less than human. Granted, Muslim men are also curtailed by fundamentalist authorities. They have no more right to broadcast interviews expressing novel opinions than women have the right to participate in them. But the traditions that the fundamentalist leaders defend with might and main are patriarchal (blatantly sexist, many feminists would say), so the restraints are fuller on women and cut more deeply into women's humanity. In fact, what humanity is left, when a person cannot determine what she is to think, wear, or consider a viable role model? Beyond physical intimidation, the deeper threat in the fundamentalist Muslim mythology of Fatimah and womanhood is an intimidation of women's souls.

For the Ayatollah and his like, women are free only to follow the traditional prescriptions, to which they are not free to say yes or no. It is not necessary that they work through their difficulties with the prescriptions and so attain a sophisticated faith. Blind obedience is the ideal, and blind obedience is what the Ayatollah strove to enforce. Whether Muhammad ever demanded blind obedience of Fatimah is irrelevant. Whether one can ever develop a robust, fully mature faith through blind obedience is a question beyond the pale. The mythic need for both surety and the subordination of women rules the Ayatollah's day. It is a truly horrifying need, stemming from deep fissures in his psyche. People who underestimate its depth come into mortal danger, as the novelist Salman Rushdie now knows. Religious mythology may well be the most powerful force in human history. That is why it is crucial that women and men cooperate to make it healthy.

5

Recent Oral Cultures

SEDNA

Eskimos of northern Canada have long recited a myth of Sedna, goddess of the sea and source of the sea animals. In the myth, Sedna was a handsome girl who proudly spurned prospective suitors. One spring a fulmar flew in from across the ice and wooed her. His song described the soft bearskins on which she would rest and the good food she would never lack if she became his wife. So she accepted his offer. However, the fulmar never fulfilled his promises, so the new bride found herself languishing in the most wretched conditions and lamenting her rejection of so many human suitors.

To avenge Sedna, her father killed the lying fulmar, but this made him and Sedna the object of the other fulmars' wrath. While Sedna and her father were fleeing from this wrath, a heavy storm arose that threatened their boat. Her father decided to surrender Sedna to the birds and threw her overboard. She clung to the side of the boat, but he cut off her fingers. The first joints became whales, the second joints became seals, and the stumps became the ground animals. The storm finally subsided, and Sedna came back into the boat, but a fierce hatred raged in her heart. So she waited until her father fell asleep, and then she had her dogs gnaw off his hands and feet. Awakening, he cursed her, the dogs, and his own wretched fate. Thereupon, the earth opened and swallowed them all. Ever since, they have lived in the underworld, where Sedna serves as mistress of the animals that move in the sea.

In Greenland, a different version of this myth depicts the goddess of the sea as an old woman. She lives on the ocean floor, sitting in her house before an oil lamp and sending out the animals that Eskimos hunt. Usually she is generous, but sometimes parasites settle on her head and make her angry, so she holds back the game. Then the shaman must journey to the bottom of the sea to remove the parasites and restore the game. This is a perilous journey. He must cross a turning wheel of ice, negotiate a kettle of boiling water, cross a bridge as narrow as the edge of a knife, and avoid the terrible animals that guard the old woman's door. Once inside her house, he must persuade her to let him comb out her hair and remove the parasites. Only then can the people expect to regain prosperity.[1]

Sedna, or the Old Woman at the bottom of the sea, functions as a mother goddess. When Native Americans of the far north thought about the source of the seals and the fish, they envisioned a primal mother. The Old Woman is femininity somehow multiplied by being aged, long experienced in the provision of the wherewithal for survival. If many cultures represent sacral femininity as a robust, fertile mother, many others include the aged female, who has accumulated wisdom throughout a long life and so can offer spiritual as well as physical fertility and nourishment.

The vulnerability of the Old Woman to parasites is a figure for what can go wrong with the fecundity of the world. Because they found parasites in many of the fish that they caught, Eskimos imagined that the source of sea life could also become riddled and weakened. As well, the parasites could symbolize human failures. For example, if people failed to keep the taboos that custom imposed, they could weaken their relations with the source of the game—perhaps even weaken that source itself. If they hunted out of season or injured one another in brawls or performed abortions, they could throw the "system" of nature out of kilter. That system was a living network of physical and spiritual relationships. One had, for instance, to hunt properly, which was a matter of both physical techniques and spiritual attitudes.

We should not imagine oral peoples as inevitably more virtuous than peoples of larger-scale groups, but we should imagine them as more sensitive to the natural environment. Both survival and maturation toward integrity, wisdom, and holiness required an attunement to the ways and desires of nature. Nature was not merely the physical side of the seasons, the plants, and the animals. It was also the source of life, beauty, and significance. Nature gave messages to human beings. The spiritual depths of nature invited human beings to come into harmony. When the game failed or plague afflicted the tribe, something must have destroyed such harmony. Often the spiritual leader of the tribe, the shaman, found that someone had broken the moral code. Such destructive behavior required repair, for example by journeying in spirit to the Old Woman of the sea and begging her forgiveness.

The account of the origin of the sea animals from the fingers of Sedna associates the wealth of the sea with the body of the maternal goddess. From her substance came the means of Eskimo survival. This myth is more explanatory than the second, and less practical. It does not stipulate actions that the people must take (such as sending the shaman to the Old Woman) when they come into trouble. But it does provide a rationale for both the origin of the sea animals and the fickleness of nature's providing them. Sedna is permanently, perhaps intrinsically, angered because of her father's abuse. She may feel guilty that she had her dogs take revenge, but her most basic emotion is a strong resentment that her life went so badly. Had she been less proud, she might have found a good, generous husband. Had the fulmar told the truth and kept his promises, she might have enjoyed luxury. And had her father loved her more than he feared the wrath of the other fulmars, both she and he might have escaped being swallowed up by the earth. So Sedna has the consciousness of a woman wronged. Though she is not without guilt, she can think that she has been victimized. That is bound to make her provision of the sea animals uncertain. It is bound to complicate relations with her. She is the capricious, worrisome face of ultimate reality—the divinity that is sensitive, touchy, easily offended.

We should also note that the myth of Sedna suggests tangled relations between human beings and the nonhuman animals. The fulmars are at odds with Sedna and her father. The harmony that ought to obtain among heaven, earth, and the sea has cracked. Sedna lives under the sea because the people of the air, the birds, have ruined her life on earth. The otherness of birds and human beings proved to be stronger than their sameness. Certainly Sedna has her faithful dogs, but the general impact of the myth is to suggest alienation between human beings and the animal world. Life is a constant struggle, and often human beings and animals find themselves enemies.

We do not know who first composed the myth of Sedna or the myth of the Old Woman at the bottom of the sea. Eskimo culture is somewhat patriarchal, but nothing from recent history suggests that a woman could not have been the original myth-maker. Whatever the source, we should note the ambivalence about female nature expressed in both myths. The goddess is touchy. Dealing with her successfully requires considerable diplomatic skill. She lives apart from human beings, not completely happy about her isolation. Whatever satisfaction she gains from providing food and the other necessities of life is not free of regrets and irritations. She can feel put upon, burdened, and so turn uncooperative. This depiction reflects the cross-cultural stereotype that women fight emotionally, using moods and sensitivities to gain attention or get their way. Unable physically to dominate men, they turn to emotional manipulation. If they can make men feel guilty or force them to wait on female approval, they can right the balance of power, perhaps even control it.

Like most stereotypes, this depiction has its truths and its falsehoods. The safest procedure, certainly, is to go case by case, making certain that no loose generalizations determine how one views a given woman or a given relationship between a woman and a man. Still, it is useful to reflect on the way that women tend to fight for parity with men, if only because it reminds us how complicated heterosexual relations have become. After millennia of trying to live together, men and women have many reasons to wonder whether equality, and so healthy love, has ever been possible. When it is simply a fact that a given man and woman truly love one another, however, they can cut through a thousand difficulties in a flash.

The wonder is this fact: love does keep springing up, generation after generation. No stereotypes or ideologies manage to defeat it. It flows from more primordial layers of the psyche, and it finds considerable support in the practical arrangements that have arisen through the millennia. These ensure that most men need women, and vice versa. At the most basic level, men need women for children. Closely tied to this, in most cultures throughout history, is the dependence of most men on women for food and clothing. The majority of oral peoples, our present concern, have lived by hunting and gathering. Men have hunted, women have gathered—but also cooked, sewed, nursed, and maintained the living space. Men have profited greatly from women's domestic services, but women have found ways to make such services fulfilling. Just as they have taught themselves to enjoy sexual intercourse and childrearing, so most women have learned to enjoy cooking and sewing, if not cleaning. Most have found aesthetic pleasures in such work, as well as the satisfaction of knowing that their contributions to their family and the tribe were crucial to survival. Without the services of women, life could not have gone on. Without the generosity of women, life would have become much duller, taking the bloom from the rose.

The pathos of modern and postmodern cultures is that both sexes have lost any easy assurance that their labors and interactions are worthwhile. Women have found it harder and harder to believe that childrearing and homemaking justified their existence. Men have gotten more and more distracted by work and the public sphere, tending to consider home merely a way station, a place to sleep and refuel. Children have lost the support of two happily cooperative parents, as well as the support of an extended family. The possibilities opened by modern technology have taken humanity away from its simple roots in food and sex, nourishment and love.

So, however skewed or partial the imagery that we find in myths of Sedna, we may applaud their firm grasp of fundamentals. Women, especially, should reexamine the possibility of taking satisfaction in the roles that biology and social history have assigned them. Without denying their right to participate in the public spheres of work, politics, art, science, education, medicine, and whatever else appeals to them, they will be wise to think again about the pleasures and necessities of lovemaking, cooking, providing clothing, teaching children, and caring for their family's health. We human beings are not free to create the entire justification of our lives from our own intentions. We are free to retain a great say about what we consider worthwhile—how we define our contribution to the common good, the next generation, the people come close to us in love, and the gratitude humanity owes the God of creation, who made us in this strange, wonderful fashion we call being human.

THE BUFFALO MAIDEN

In 1947 the late Joseph Epes Brown, destined to become the dean of white scholars of American Indian religion, lived with an old member of the Oglala Sioux, Black Elk, through a harsh South Dakota winter. Through numerous conversations, Black Elk imparted to Brown the basic outline of his people's culture. The main rites that Black Elk described were seven ceremonies communicated to the Sioux (Lakota) in the primeval past by the Buffalo Maiden, a lovely young woman who represented the holiness of both the creative powers and the buffalo, on whom the Sioux depended.

The myth of the Buffalo Maiden, handed down as a tradition kept by the remote ancestors to whom she had first appeared, impressed upon the Sioux their obligation to keep sacred the pipe that offered them a way to communicate with heaven. The *wakan* (holy) powers responsible for life would respond to the rising of the smoke of the shared pipe, when the smokers purified their hearts and sent their spirits along with the smoke. The smoke was like the breath of life, like the wind that came from all four directions. It was like the inspirations that moved the mind, the sense of togetherness that knit the people together. The spirit of the people, that which quickened them to wisdom and courage, was the most important part of their culture. The rites imparted by the Buffalo Maiden gave the Sioux people a system of sacraments through which to train their spirits and express them beautifully.[2]

The Lakota associated their goddess with the buffalo because this animal was their main source of food and clothing. What the seal was to the coastal Eskimo, the buffalo was to the Plains Indians. No portion of the buffalo went unused. Certainly the Lakota and other tribes drew on other sources of food, other materials from which to construct their houses and protect themselves against heat and cold. But the buffalo, so impressive and plentiful, was the crux of traditional, prewhite economics on the Plains. Thus the decimation of the buffalo by whites spelled the end of traditional Plains culture. Once the animal that had been both the substance and the symbol of their long-standing way of life passed from the scene, the traditional Plains Indians could be no more.

The seven rites that the Buffalo Maiden gave to the Lakota ancestors were (1) a ceremony for purifying the souls of the dead, (2) a ceremonial use of the sweat lodge for spiritual purification, (3) a ritual for "crying for a vision" that would illumine a person's vocation, (4) the sun dance (a sacrifice of personal pain to the sun, for the welfare of the entire tribe), (5) a ritual for making outsiders into relatives (i.e., members of the tribe), (6) a consecration of a girl come into sexual maturity, and (7) a sacred ball game that represented the place of human beings

in the awesome scheme of the cosmos. In most of these ceremonies one could use the sacred pipe. Collectively, the seven rites
offered the Sioux a system through which to consecrate every
bit of personal and social life. The prayers of the various rituals
drew the entirety of nature into the people's prayers of thanks-
giving and petition. Again and again the smoke of the pipe arose
as a sign of both gratitude and need.

What should we make of this Native American chapter in
the mythology of sacral womanhood? What is the significance
of the fact that the traditional rites of the Oglala Sioux came
from the hands of a mysterious holy female? First, we may muse
about the choice of a young woman. Native American culture
honored both Father Sky and Mother Earth. It tended to represent ultimate reality as a grandparental force concerned with the
well-being of humankind. Though men predominated in tribal
rule, the relations between the sexes were balanced. Women
prevailed in the spheres assigned to them. Women's power to
bring forth life both equaled and contrasted with men's power to
kill. Native American cultures tended to sharpen the differences
between the sexes, at least for the period of sexual activity. In
childhood and old age, such differences diminished. So the advent of the traditional rites must have represented a force of life,
a kind of birth and nourishment, more properly appropriated to
women than to men. The liturgical life of the people must have
seemed to lodge in something more feminine than masculine.
What could that something have been?

In extremis, human beings present themselves to ultimate
reality, their divinity, as vulnerable. In their most significant
rites, they lay bare their souls and confess the simple truth: they
are mortal, ignorant, and sinful. They are but creatures of a day,
and often they are afraid. At such times, it is comforting to
think that divinity is kindly, understanding, welcoming. Stereotypically, mothers are more kindly, understanding, and welcoming than fathers. Across cultures, women's nearly inevitable
involvement in childrearing has made theirs the face that people
seek when they need tender comforting.

Most likely, Black Elk's people sensed that their rites placed them in jeopardy. In taking up the sacred pipe, they were confessing their great need of divine help. However necessary it was for them to comport themselves rightly under the eye of heaven, they could rejoice that their stipulated ways of petitioning heaven had come from a kindly and beautiful woman. The substories about the Buffalo Maiden stress that she was completely pure. When one of the two young men to whom she first appeared felt pangs of lust for her, he entered into a fog that destroyed him. However, even though she could not be an object of sexual desire, she could be beautiful, gracious, gentle, and generous—young, fertile femininity at the peak of perfection. She could seem to live beyond human tawdriness, in the holy realms that human imagination could only glimpse now and then.

Living beyond human desire, free of the many imperfections and limitations of ordinary men (and ordinary women), the Buffalo Maiden appeared to the traditional, faithful Sioux psyche as a muse—an inspiration to stir and safeguard cultural creativity. The system of rites that her mythology both explained and inspired took its beauty from herself, its source. To bless a departed soul or consecrate the quest for a vision or go to the sweat lodge for purification was to enter again the world of ultimate realities, the zones of spirit where meaning seemed secure from all the depredations of space and time.

Sanctifying the spirits of the departed (whether old or young) allowed the Lakota to ease the pains of death and assure themselves that death was not the end of human significance. Purifying themselves in the sweat lodge allowed the Lakota to come to grips with their wrongdoings, repent, and turn again to the right path. Crying for a vision was the Sioux equivalent of Christian confirmation. A young person on the verge of adulthood could find direction, purpose, and even the raw material for a personal identity when the fasting and solitude were rewarded with the message of a spiritual helper (e.g., a bird or bear). The sun dance, perhaps the most famous Sioux ritual, sought the defense and reinvigoration of the entire "hoop" of the Sioux people. By piercing their breasts with leather thongs and dancing constantly before the blazing summer sun, the men who sacrificed themselves expressed their dedication to the well-being of the entire tribe. As well, they made a claim on the mercy and help of the sun, that great symbol of the heavenly Father overseeing all creation, assuring it light and warmth.

Similarly, the consecration of the tribe's young women sanctified the next generation. The ritual for making outsiders into relatives smoothed the way between Sioux and others they wished to befriend. And the sacred ball game introduced a note of holy play. Just as the cosmic elements went their inscrutable ways, combining and separating as the Creator had instructed them, so human beings participated in the spontaneity of creation, the kaleidoscope that changed constantly before the Creator, giving him, or her, praise and enjoyment. Each of these rituals fulfilled a significant need of the Sioux psyche. Each contributed to a sense that human existence was meaningful, beautiful, and well provisioned. Without these rituals, the Sioux might have felt naked before their enemies—death, meaninglessness, even madness. With them, they felt well-equipped to keep going on.

To speak of a sense of feeling well-equipped is to enter the domain of the psyche where feminine bounty has seemed a token of divine blessings. Again and again, it has been women who have provided the food, the infant's milk, even the flesh that created a new generation. Women are more closely identified with the creation and protection of life than are men. Thus it made psychological sense to credit the rites that created and protected Sioux culture to a beautiful young woman. It pleased the depths of the soul, where desires as deep as the beginnings of life in the womb continued to burn. And it pleased the heights of the soul, where people wanted images of beauty, purity, gentleness, and refinement.

The Buffalo Maiden is an excellent example of the mythical femininity that has shaped both male and female psyches for centuries. In her we see much of the perennial desire that human beings direct toward God. Even when they do not know what they want or from whom they want it, human beings often long to meet perfection, light and comfort that do not fail. The myth of the Buffalo Maiden allowed countless Sioux to fulfill this longing. The better we appreciate the ways that traditional cultures have created mythologies of womanhood for such fulfillment, the better we can assess the gains and losses in this process.

SOUTH AMERICAN MOTHER GODDESSES

Several traditional, oral tribes living in the Gran Chaco of South America have worshiped female deities as their supreme divinities. As well, virtually all traditional, pre-Christian South Americans have kept a place for lesser goddesses, even when their overall schema of divinity has pivoted on male deities. Let us consider the following scholarly indication of data that intimate the place of female creatorhood in one geographic area of traditional South America:

As Metraux (1946) pointed out, the missionaries who searched for belief in a supreme being among the Indians of the Gran Chaco were not at all successful. The only mythical personality who comes close to the conception of a superior god, in Metraux's opinion, is Eschetewuarha ("mother of the universe"), the dominant deity among the Chamacoco, a Samuco group in the north Chaco region. She is the mother of numerous forest spirits as well as of the clouds. As the controller of all things, Eschetewuarha ensures that mankind receives water. In return for this favor, she expects her people to send songs to her nightly, and when such expectations are not fulfilled she punishes them. Herbert Baldus (1932), who provided in-depth information about Eschetewuarha, compares her with the universal mother of the Cagaba (Koghi), a Chibcha tribe in Colombia that had been influenced by more advanced cultures. The obvious characteristics of a supreme god are apparently present in Kuma, the goddess of the Yaruro, who subsist on fishing, hunting, and gathering along the Capanaparo River, a tributary of the Orinoco in Venezuela. She is considered to be a moon goddess and consort of the sun god, who is unimportant. Kuma created the world with the help of two brothers, the Water Serpent and the Jaguar, after whom the tribal moieties were named. Although she apparently created the first two human beings herself, her son, Hatschawa, became the educator and culture hero of mankind. Kuma dominates a paradise in the west in which gigantic counterparts for every plant and animal species exist. Shamans are capable of seeing the land of Kuma in dreams and visions and are able to send their souls there. As a reliable informant explained, "Everything originated from Kuma and everything that the Yaruro do has been arranged so by her; the other gods and cultural heroes act according to her laws."[3]

For each of these beliefs, the tribe in question had a story, a myth. Thus the motherhood of Eschetewuarha, which embraced the forest spirits and the clouds, was not a doctrine so much as a subject of narratives handed down generation after generation. What made the Chamacoco fix upon Eschetewuarha lies hidden in the mysteries of their cultural origins and development. Why their specific historical experiences or ecological niches should have led them to concentrate on water is only partially recoverable. One would have to understand the entirety of Chamacoco culture to grasp the full significance of Eschetewuarha, as one would have to understand the entirety of Jewish and Hellenistic cultures in the lifetime of Jesus to grasp the full signficance of the original Christian mythology. Still, it is stimulating to think that the ultimate power in the traditional Chamacoco culture was a motherly figure who wanted her children to sing to her each evening. Why she would punish them if they failed this obligation is unclear. Was she hurt at their ingratitude or concerned for their well-being, which she knew depended on their turning to her with grateful hearts?

Kuma, the moon goddess of the Yaruro, reminds us of the traditional associations among fertility, the moon, women, and the night. The water serpent may introduce a phallic element, while the jaguar is the greatest animal of South American mythology. Indeed, when the classical Mesoamericans wanted to symbolize the kinship beween human beings and the animal world, they created "werejaguars"—figures with features of both human beings and jaguars. The paradise of Kuma in the West, which shamans can visit, probably comes from the human instinct that there must be something beyond the setting of the sun that preserves and fulfills the course the sun travels each day. If so, then the periodization of our human time is not the prison of our desires. There is a place where the "more" in us will be fulfilled.

Naturally, the rising moon is associated with the setting of the sun. Speculating with the dreamy freedom that traditional oral cultures often encouraged, the Yaruro might have thought the goddess of the moon the natural deity to preside over the western paradise. Indeed, when they concluded that this paradise or realer place had to contain the archetypes of all living things, they might have wanted the divinity presiding there to be a great mother, the womb of all living things.

The possible combinations of female and male aspects of creation are endless. The history of the world's religions reveals an endless cultural fertility. If the majority of supreme gods are male, the most likely reason is the predominance of patriarchy. Men have ruled most human groups. This does not imply that tribes that made a female figure supreme were not patriarchal. It simply suggests that seeing supreme human authority vested in male figures tended to make women as well as men vest supreme divine authority in male figures. But the fallible character of male rule in human affairs and the amazing power of female fertility could offset this tendency. There was no necessary attribution of divine supremacy to either male or female figures. Many traditional peoples apparently thought that the ultimate character of divinity lay beyond human reckoning and so was hinted best by a proliferation of figures.

The theologies of the high Western religions have confirmed some of this instinct. Judaism, Christianity, and Islam, all claiming to derive from divine revelation, have tended to picture the divinity as male but refrained from making such a picture requisite. Their "God" has always stood beyond sexual representation. Indeed, Judaism and Islam have opposed representing the divine through any finite forms, while Christian theology has taught that God is at most analogous to what human beings can experience—somewhat like it, but more profoundly unlike it. The proper conclusion from the Jewish, Christian, and Muslim theologies, then, is that when we speak of divinity, as we must, we should take pains to stress the mysteriousness, the otherness of ultimate reality. Similarly, when we choose to speak of characteristics based on human sexual differences, we should take pains to avoid identifying the divine with either male or female qualities. Just as Hindu iconography has often presented leading divinities as androgynous, so the high Western theologies have placed God beyond sexual limitation. Similarly, most tribal peoples of South America have given the gods consorts, insisting in another way that male-femaleness, a conjoint representation of human features, is the best analogy for divinity.

I have been belaboring this point about the proper imagining of ultimate reality because it leaps from the pages when one studies continental areas such as South America. The standard message in the areas not shaped by the Jewish, Christian, and Muslim faiths has been that anything, if not everything, reflects the divine. Now this and now that may focus the awesome power of the Creator, as well as the obvious need of human beings for a Savior and Judge beyond finite measures. A subpoint in this message is that female characteristics are essential to our proper imagining of the divinity. When we ask about the likeness of God to ourselves, knowing intuitively that if God is wholly unlike us there can be no communion between us and God, we have to keep maleness and femaleness on the same level—we have to make them equally near to and far from the nature of God.

It is a radical defect of the Jewish, Christian, and Muslim religious cultures that they have not obeyed this imperative, thus ignoring what the history of traditional South American, North American, African, or Asian religions makes plain. Certainly, they have their own reasons for male supremacy, rooted in their own patriarchal histories of revelation. Yet they have tolerated, if not encouraged, a destructive dissonance between the core of their message about God and their popular theology, morality, ritual, and mythology.

At the core they have said that God is as close to femininity as to masculinity, but throughout their cultural extensions they have made masculinity more highly valued. Certainly it would be quixotic to think that a little exposure to different religious creations, such as the cultures of the traditional tribes of the Gran Chaco, would have given the creators of the Jewish, Christian, and Muslim cultures serious pause. But feminists can take heart from the simple fact that the patriarchal theologies of the originally Near Eastern religions have been only part of the overall, global story. The feminists' God more sympathetic to feminine qualities has not left herself without strong witness. Thus feminists can use the mythologies of supreme goddesses like those of Gran Chaco to spotlight the peculiar, not necessarily regulative, character of the geneses of canonical myths in Judaism, Christianity, and Islam, and so require a truly critical understanding of revelation in these three religions.

For example, can it be an essential part of divine revelation to misstate the relations between the sexes or the shares that the sexes have in the proper symbolism for God? Does what separates "higher" monotheistic religions from those of the traditional Gran Chaco necessarily include a theological male chauvinism? Or do the symbolisms of the Jewish, Christian, and Muslim deities admit of a revisionist theological impulse that would break down the masculine hegemony traditionally excluding equal status for feminine analogies?

Judaism and Islam would seem easier cases for feminists to handle than Christianity, inasmuch as they deny a historical incarnation of ultimate reality in male form. The Christian teaching about the Incarnation of the Logos that brought about

Jesus of Nazareth offers more difficulties, but these are insuperable only if one insists that the Incarnation had to occur in a male form. If one can hold that, other cultural conditions warranting, the Word made flesh could have been a female, the Christian doctrine of the Incarnation is not intrinsically male chauvinistic.

I see no reason why one cannot hold this position. I find nothing in the canonical understanding of the Trinitarian relations to necessitate the Incarnation of the Second Person as a male. So I do not find Christianity intrinsically male chauvinistic, irredeemably sexist.

I believe that this finding is enough to save Christianity from necessary rejection by feminists and keep its theology open to extra-Christian wisdoms, including such apparently lowly ones as those fashioned by small tribes of illiterate children of God living in the Gran Chaco. One can lament the historical development of Christian male chauvinism and demand that the churches cast out their current sexist practices, but one need not judge Christianity immured against lessons that its own God has long offered peoples outside its historical pale. One can judge Christianity redeemable, able in principle to learn as well as teach, and so one can hope that some day the beauties of sacral femininity will be as plain to Christians as those of sacral masculinity.

THE YORUBA OSHUN

The traditional Yoruba of present-day Nigeria celebrate an attractive goddess, Oshun, associated with the river bearing her name. She has figured in both the traditional conception of the operations of the natural world, including those underscored by farming, and in the traditional rituals through which the Yoruba have contacted their *orisha* (divinities). A revealing song to Oshun speaks of her as possessing a velvet skin bedecked in brass and parrot feathers. Cowrie shells adorn her black buttocks, and her eyes sparkle like the sun on the river. The wisdom of the forest and the river reposes in her. She is the ultimate source of the doctor's power to heal, since she provides the fresh water that is the best medicine. When she cures children, through her ritual activity, she works freely, asking no payment. Dry, barren women may go to her for help. Often they will return juicy as a ripe palm fruit. There is nothing sweeter than the touch of a child's hand; Oshun-the-fertile gives children generously.[4]

The headwaters of the Oshun River run quickly, providing cool, clean, liquid refeshment. They are the natural source of the symbolism surrounding the goddess. She is quick, playful, beautiful, cheerful. One myth explains the extension of her domain from the Oshun River to all waterways, including the oceans. Her father became jealous of the love that Oshun's beauty created in all the creatures of the river. He fought against this jealously, but finally it became too much for him, so he moved against her. She fled for her life to the depth of the river, where she found egress to the primal ocean—the source of all waterways. Eventually her father repented of his jealousy, and they were reunited, but her travels had made her mistress of all rivers and seas.

Her lively personality, along with her beauty, makes Oshun an unrepentant flirt. She is always getting involved with males, teasing them, loving sexual byplay. She has married many different gods, but none has been able to hold her. Once one of these gods set a trap for her. Suspecting her of infidelity, he trained his parakeets to spy on her movements. When she found that they were singing about her affairs, Oshun gave them a fiery rum. Drunk, they slurred their words so that their songs came out, "Oshun is full of virtue. She never leaves the house." This ruse ultimately failed, however, and Oshun was exposed as unfaithful. Still, she never fully repented, and to this day she is cheerfully promiscuous, a happy, saintly whore.

This is an interesting mythology. It brims with life, and even when it is questionable morally, it brings out an attractive side of feminine potential. Women have often been portrayed as more playful than men, and more sensual. Where men have had to carry the gravity of rule, tribal authority, women have been free to cut up, providing a lightening balance. Also, their closer association with children has made playfulness useful to women. They have found they could make their children happier if they retained a lively capacity for play, imagination, and laughter.

Certainly, there are other stereotypes, including those that make femininity closer to wisdom than masculinity. Women have often symbolized the purity and detachment that wisdom requires, if it is to stand free of passing passions. But many mythologies reconcile these two sets of qualities by making wisdom itself playful. The ultimate ordering of the world is not an onerous, grim business. To be worthy of God, creation must proceed easily, delightfully, dancingly.

This is the implication of the Indian *lila,* the play that makes creation both an illusion and a delight. It is the implication of the biblical figure of Lady Wisdom playing before God at creation, delighting him (Prov. 8:30–31). Oshun makes this intuition earthier, but she is akin to the other goddesses of play. In her figure traditional Yoruba could find many reasons to laugh, look upon creation as a beauty provided for their enjoyment, delight in the vitality of a healthy human nature.

Such a vitality is bound to include sexual pleasure and alertness. Oshun represents the rush of energy that comes when people fall in love. She suggests the renewal of youth created by love, as well as the excesses that chasing pleasure can bring. While her main profile is attractive, there are cautionary features. The train of jealous lovers in her wake suggests pain, even violence. Overall, however, she endorses life in the body, life close to the earth. "It is good to feel charged with life, desire, playfulness," she preaches. She is young, perhaps eternally so, and she has yet to suffer. But suffering will come soon enough. For the moment, people do well to appreciate the joy that she offers.

Women, especially, do well to appreciate the vitality available in their beautiful bodies. They do well to look upon physical love as an enticing art. Time will show them the limits of this perspective. Aging and sickness will teach them other, complementary lessons. But these later lessons will swell out of proportion unless youth has had its day. Life will seem only pain and trouble unless love has taken them out of themselves, made them giddy with joy and energy.

Few goddesses represent this message as brazenly, as unqualifiedly, as Oshun. Few call to mind a time of life, a place on the earth, as quick and dancing as hers. In later chapters of her mythology, Oshun becomes the mother of numerous children. However, the main mythological accent continues to fall on her youth. Catholic Nigerians have sometimes transmuted her into the mother of the Christ child, still beautiful and joyous but purified of all wantonness. The extension of both her maternal affection and her lively flirtatiousness into love of her devotees has sealed her appeal. In the final analysis, she is not aflush with desire and life selfishly. She wants to share her joy with all who come to her in petition. She wants to lighten their burdens, turn their tears into smiles.

What is the balance that feminine self-understanding ought to seek? Where lies the golden mean between sensuality and spirituality, love of life's pleasures and discipline of desire because it easily goes astray? These questions are not peculiar to women. The history of asceticism the world over shows that they have preoccupied monks and yogins even more. But they remain valid queries, probes that women have to keep putting to themselves if they are to estimate rightly their own embodiment, to learn for themselves the blend of indulgence and restraint that God asks. Agreed, there is no single formula applicable to all women, or even suitable for all phases of the life cycle. Probably, young women need to learn the typical effects of sexual play by letting a healthy, attractive body express an amused, interesting persona. Probably, older women ought to reflect on the implications of the failure of pleasure to sustain a spiritual life, without turning away from the beauty of the world or the goodness of sexual love. For everything there is a season.

Still, from Oshun I have drawn what I hope are profitable images of a playfulness, an ineffable lightness of being, that need not conflict with an inner awareness, even a spiritual readiness to let go of the play, when serious or painful matters intrude. Without playfulness, we cannot give to our Creator the full measure of praise that the goodness of creation warrants and solicits. Without laughter and yea-saying, we deny the glint of the sun off the waters, the race of the blood in love, and so we are not truthful in our nightly addresses of God.

The burble of the headwaters of the Oshun is like the music of the glorified soul, brought fully alive by the love of God, which goes to the depths of creation to give the numbers, the molecular statistics, their marching orders. The glorified soul, embraced by God and stabilized in the joy of the divine mystery, senses how creation itself is a divine play. Taken beyond death and history, speaking from the extrapolated viewpoint of heaven, the glorified soul can see the pathos of creation in a new light. In Christian terms, the crucifixion stands at the center of a new, higher constellation of events, while the sin that necessitated it becomes a happy fault. All responsible people rush to say that this higher viewpoint does not make evil good or minimize horrible sufferings. Nonetheless, when meeting the joy of an Oshun or contemplating the faces of little children at Easter, one can sense the warrants for the orthodox Christian assurance that all things will be well.

All things are well if they are held by a divinity that enters the marrow of human experience, embracing both its sorrows and its joys. All things are well if divinity expresses itself in the dazzling smile of an Oshun, as well as the sufferings of Christ. The great benefit of studying the mythologies of the world religions is that one finds *all* aspects of human experience sanctified. Nothing important to women or men has been neglected. Whatever human beings have found interesting, beautiful, needing redemption, crying out for redress, or calling them to worship points to the one God, the sole divine force responsible for the mystery of creation.

Oshun, like the Greek god Dionysius, expresses the joyous sacredness of the life-force. With a wicked humor and a devastating flirtatiousness and wit, she draws her followers to her in earthy laughter. Theologians have to find a place for this intuition about the ultimate nature of God. Unless their conception of the holy reality from which everything positive issues is to fail some of the most delightful human experiences, God must be like an Oshun, beckoning us to playful intimacy. Otherwise, God is much duller than our myths. Otherwise, the Creator is less interesting than the creation. That cannot be. For God to be God, divinity must always be more.

THE RAINBOW SNAKE

Native Australian mythology gives a prominent place to a female divinity depicted as the rainbow snake that arches in the heavens after a storm.

In one traditional western Arnhem Land view the Rainbow Snake is a creator, the first mother. She travels under the sea from the northwest, and on the mainland she eventually gives birth to the people she is carrying inside her. She vomits them out, licking them with her tongue to make them grow and scraping them with mussel shells to make their skin smooth and lighter in color. Some Gunwinggu women have told me: "No matter what [our social affiliation] we call her *gagag*, 'mother's mother.' We live on the ground, she lives underneath, inside the ground and in the water[s]. She urinated fresh water for us to drink, otherwise we would all have died of thirst. She showed us what foods to collect. She vomited the first people, the Dreaming people, who prepared the country for us, and she made us, so that we have minds and sense to understand. She gave us our [social categories and] language, she made our tongues and teeth and throats and breath: she shared her breath with us, she gave us breath, from when we first sat inside our mothers' wombs. She looks a bit like a woman, and a bit like a snake."[5]

Let us first assimilate this description and then reflect on it as a final contribution to the mythology of women that we have been studying across the span of humanity's religious cultures. Note, first, that the Rainbow Snake is not the sole deity, not even the sole creative deity. Other parts of this anthropological report make it clear that in aboriginal Australian cultures the roster of gods and goddesses varies from locale to locale. Some peoples pay more attention to the Rainbow Snake, others pay less. Nonetheless, the reputable scholar A. R. Radcliffe-Brown, writing in 1930, expressed the opinion that the Rainbow Snake was perhaps the most important of the native divinities drawn from the powers of nature.[6]

To call the Rainbow Snake the first mother is to suggest that there are other mothers, perhaps both divine and human. Certainly the rest of the account that we are analyzing, drawn from interviews with native Australian women, assimilates the motherhood of the Rainbow Snake to that of human mothers. Part of the bounty that the informants see in the Rainbow Snake derives from her having done for human beings even more than human mothers can do for their children. The journey of the Rainbow Snake under the sea from the Northwest reflects the traditional cosmology, which pictures the land surrounded by primeval waters. It may also reflect the ability of snakes to swim as well as the arc of the rainbow over the ocean to the end of the horizon. The Rainbow Snake is carrying "people" inside her. These include the first human beings, but perhaps also the other creatures. (Many oral peoples do not maintain a sharp distinction between human beings and animals, and most oral mythologies attribute personal qualities to animals, including speech and the ability to think and feel.)

Human beings are born on the land, suggesting that land, rather than water, is their original and so proper habitat. (Some other peoples' mythologies postulate an origin in the waters.) The birth is by the Rainbow Snake's vomiting them forth, which may suggest a kinship between human beings and the divine "mouth"—that is, what divinity has to say. The mouth could be more dignified than the vagina, though vomiting is not an origin calculated to make human beings feel proud. The licking of the first people likens the Rainbow Snake to an animal mother, concerned to cleanse her new offspring. How it would make them grow is not clear, unless again the oral motif suggests speech, communication, the education by which humanity becomes more specifically human. Probably native Australians themselves used mussel shells for various scraping operations. Why making the first human beings lighter in color would be desirable is hard to say. Perhaps differences in skin pigment introduced a color consciousness early in aboriginal history. This would only have increased with the advent of whites in the eighteenth century.

The report of the Gunwinggu women personalizes the snake goddess. She is not just an abstract deity but someone to whom these women feel related. Devotion to her cuts across all sociological differences. (Aboriginal tribes were conscious of bloodlines, which had much to say about who could marry whom.) To call the Rainbow Snake "mother's mother" was to place her at the origin of all fertility. She was the source of the ancestors, the font of motherhood itself. This generic provision of life is balanced by specific, humble gifts. Although human beings live on the ground and the Snake lives under the ground or in the waters, she has cared for their land-based life by providing water and knowledge of foods. That the water came from her own body suggests that she is indeed a cosmic creator. The primal elements have derived from her being.

In showing the people what foods to collect, the Rainbow Snake acted like a culture hero. Scholars sometimes distinguish between creators and culture heroes. The former fashion the cosmos, while the later instruct human beings in what is necessary for survival or what have become staples of tribal culture. A knowledge of the edible plants and animals of a given area is absolutely essential for survival and so ranks high on the list of what oral peoples usually attribute to their culture heroes. Since women have often been the primary gatherers, their traditional expertise has tended to focus on plants, roots, and berries. Relatedly, women have been the experts in not only the nutritional value of these potential foods but also their healing qualities.

The Dreaming people were the first human beings to inhabit the landscape. By naming the different features, they organized the human world. Even today, aboriginal Australians are great students of local landscapes. Each significant item has its own story, for each came to be dramatically, in the Dream-time. Typically, native peoples carry in their heads a sophisticated map of their home region. Regularly, they sing the myths explaining the origins of the different features, and such singing relates them to the ancestors of the Dream-time.

Overall, the traditional conception of spiritual maturation has understood it to be a progressive entry into the Dream-time. Thus, human existence could be schematized as a circle. People originated from the ancestors, coming out of the Dream-time (the chaos that creativity requires, before it establishes order). As they grew from childhood to adulthood, their interest in tribal lore was supposed to make them desire more and more to contemplate the Dream-time. In part this was a preparation for death, when one would return to the ancestors and enjoy the land as it had been when newly created—when it was most beautiful. In part it was a focus for contemplative wisdom, sanctioning the native desire to imagine what seemed most real and attractive in the tribal mythology.

The Dreaming people begotten by the Rainbow Snake prepared the land, but the Rainbow Snake herself gave the people their minds. It was her doing that human beings should be able to understand their situations, have cultures and languages. As well, she provided the sociological classifications that the tribes now use. Thus the Rainbow Serpent is no absent deity, responsible only for the first phases of an evolutionary process. She may be sensed in all specifically human activity, including thought, social life, and language. She is also responsible for the people's physical well-being, involving their tongues, teeth, throats, and breath. The continuance of the oral imagery strengthens the suspicion that the mouth, source of the most compelling human significance, has held a special place in the mythological physiology of aboriginal Australians. Combined with the breath, provision for the mouth suggests a care for the entirety of human existence: both physical being and mental capacity.

Finally, the appearance of the Rainbow Snake as like a woman and like a snake symbolizes the analogy of being latent in this, as most other, accounts of the Creator. The Rainbow Snake, the primal mother, is both like and unlike the women reflecting on her bounty. She is a woman like them—a mother, a rational creature, a source of life and care. But she is also not like them. She pertains more to the nonhuman world than they do. She exhibits the mystery of purer animality, less rational and so perhaps more primal being. Indeed, her associations with the rainbow give her a celestial dimension, as her mythical connections with the seas give her an oceanic dimension. She is cosmic, as well as akin to human beings. She is other, and so awesome, sacred, one before whom human beings ought to bow. Her divinity appears most exactly in this otherness. She is sacred, more profoundly real than any of the creatures she has brought forth, and so it is legitimate, even imperative, to worship her.

What do we seek when we worship our divinities? What is the self-knowledge we may discover if we probe genuine prayer? For native Australians, the answer would include a powerful affirmation of feminine creativity. The women interviewed about the Rainbow Snake were grateful to live in the patterns established by the mother's mother. Certainly, their worship was not simply honoring themselves, a legitimated narcissism. It expressed awe at the mysteriousness of creation. But one benefit of worshiping this mysteriousness in the form of the Rainbow Snake was to find their own portion in the Creator ratified. What had made them was wonderful, and in consequence what they themselves were was wonderful. We find a similar pattern in the Bible. Worshiping the Creator leads the psalmist to declaim the marvels of his or her own creation: what a thing is human nature!

I am reluctant to develop this insight, lest I give false signals. A psychological age seeks signs of self-worth everywhere, and many that it finds are problematic. The center of worship is not ourselves but God. The source of true mental health is not our own psyches but the objective splendor of God's creation. God's love for us is gratuitous, not something we are owed. We are not by nature depraved, but neither are we our own fulfillment. The love that makes us whole goes far beyond our healing. The heaven to which we aspire is much more than our own completion. Always, we are partial and only God is whole. Always, we must decrease and God increase, if truth is to be served. One of the most devastating losses we can trace to modernity is the eclipse of this truth. Paradoxically, we are more needy because less cosmological, more psychological. Paradoxically, much of the wisdom we need to reestablish right relations with our selves, as well as the natural environment, lies ready to hand in the myths of premodern peoples.

6

Conclusion

MYTHOLOGICAL WOMAN

We have surveyed some of the data relevant to estimating the significance of the mythologies of women that we find in the world's religions. From prehistoric, Asian, originally Near Eastern, and recent oral traditions we have noted the impact of women's fertility, beauty, difference from men, and numerous other noteworthy characteristics. It would be perilous to attempt to summarize what our survey has implied, to say nothing of what our survey could only suggest has been the full story of women's appearance in the human psyche, when that psyche has grappled with ultimate reality. Thus our present task is merely to revisit the data briefly, to recall the main patterns we found.

For Old Europe, we apprenticed ourselves to Marija Gimbutas, following her fascination with chevrons and V-symbols, trying to grasp the messages encoded in statues like those of the stiff white lady. For classical Greece, which loomed as a mythological culture especially rich in allusions to feminine characteristics, we reflected on the stories of Hera and Artemis, where the abstract communication of Old Europe yielded to more personal interests.

If we pause at this point, the following generalization comes to mind. The mythology of women that one finds in the world religions swings between these two poles. The abstract or generic, where the stimulus is usually the fertility of women, has predominated, but the personal has also made an impact. Living apart from history, thinking of themselves as more immersed in the cycles of nature than dominating them, the majority of our ancestors have concentrated on the essential features of their condition. When they have tried to cast their explanatory intuitions into stories, they have lingered over what might illumine death itself, life itself, animality itself, womanhood itself. The death of a given elder, the birth of a given infant, the power of a given jaguar, the beauty of a given girl might be implied in their stories or be called to mind, but usually the storytellers have anticipated Plato in realizing that what makes us human is our power to generalize; what offers the explanations we need to rise above the daily flux is our power to abstract.

Probably this power always was fresh enough to elicit wonder. Or maybe the storytellers were only dimly aware that their ambition actually reached toward understanding the human condition globally. Either way, we find the majority of traditional accounts of both human existence and the nature of women concerned with general features. On the whole, their art has yet to personalize the quest for wisdom, to think that studying elder A or infant B in detail would be the best way to understand death or life.

Certainly, Hera, Artemis, and the other goddesses of classical Greece represent a step toward the modern Western desire to personalize the search for understanding. Similarly, Asian goddesses such as Kali bridge the way between a given instance of sacred femininity and sacred femininity itself. But the accent remains predominantly impersonal. Little of the soap opera wafts through traditional religious mythology. Regularly the focus is how the world itself functions, what the powers governing the world themselves are like. The human players in the dramatic stories remain small, relatively incidental.

This remained the case where the abstract seems to have been personalized to make it approachable, as, for example, when

Buddhists imagined the Prajnaparamita as a goddess. There the concern with ultimate wisdom itself far overshadowed any personal attributes that Lady Wisdom might manifest. We find a few more personal attributes in the mythologies of the Japanese sun goddess Amaterasu and the Indian goddess Radha, but hardly anything to tempt us to locate sacred femininity in actual history. In both cases the archetypal is far more significant than the concrete or particular. The traditional Chinese veneration of the moon is further support for this characterization, as is the traditional Tibetan veneration of Tara.

Moreover, if we try to take seriously stories of meetings between supposedly human females and divinities, we find that the human females are often put into impossible situations, inescapable double binds. This adds to our impression that the narratives are not much interested in illuminating the idiosyncrasies of actual human experience or personhood. The traditional myths think they have bigger fish to fry: how things stand for all human beings, what context any woman or man has to understand if she or he is to survive. Incontestably, Hindu mythology is more comfortable with a sacral female such as Laksmi than a supposedly historical woman such as Anasuya, the wife of an actual sage, and the other Asian mythologies agree with the Hindu on this point.

The accent begins to change, the atmosphere to vary, when we enter the orbit of originally Near Eastern religious mythology, but not so greatly that one can clearly foresee modern Western personalism. The Sumerian Inanna, for example, is more a generic representation of female sexuality than a woman interesting for her individual characteristics or experiences. She is more the type against which all women might be measured than an individual varying from the generically female type. Her sensuality is probably greater than that of the typical Asian goddess, but some Indian sacred females are nearly as erotic.

Isis, the Egyptian goddess we studied, is more maternal than erotic, and perhaps it is significant that she is more closely identified with wisdom than was Inanna, as though to suggest that motherhood has more to do with gaining proper perspective than sexual heat. The Gnostic Sophia is virtually by definition a figure for wisdom. The only interesting sexual overtones in her cult come from the implication that wisdom itself is androgynous: an inextricable femaleness remains, even when social or intellectual structures favor maleness.

Lilith, the Jewish demonness, carries dark associations with death, somewhat like Kali, but her sexuality introduces an interesting quirk. In wanting to be independent of male control, she expresses some telltale rebellious features in the Jewish female psyche, some murmurs against rabbinic patriarchy. But the result of her revolt—her becoming a fearsome force for evil—carried the message that such murmurs were deadly dangerous, a mythological communication that is quite daunting. To balance it, Jews could contemplate the divinization of femininity in the figure of the Shekhinah. There traditional Judaism made its apologies to the femaleness it had denigrated in creating Lilith and put a gracious womanliness within the reality of the Holy itself.

The medieval Christian willingness to feminize Jesus suggests a similar desire to make amends for patriarchal excesses. When they contemplated the goodness of God, mystics such as Julian of Norwich did not hesitate to make divinity maternal. Indeed, they did not hesitate to cross historical genders and make Jesus the mother of Christians' spiritual life. This suggests how powerful the mythical impulse can be. To override the foundations of a religion glorifying in its historicity, the medieval imagination had in effect to argue that the enfleshment of divinity included the most tender feminine emotions. If it did not, divinity would not be credible as the best of all loves.

Some of the same dynamics, much of the same insistence, attaches to the figure of the Virgin Mary. Although the high Christian tradition never countenanced according her a divine status, the folk tradition, where the mythical imagination was less fettered by dogma, treated Mary like a mother goddess.

The Qur'an, in contrast, presents Mary as only a paradigmatic instance of Muslim faith. She cannot be a partaker of divinity, as Jesus and Muhammad cannot, because God is absolutely unique, sharing divinity with nothing outside the godhead. Still, for the Qur'an to make Mary a paradigm of faith is enormously significant, because it puts limits to Muslim patriarchy and shows that women can be as favored by God as men. The Qur'an never treats Fatimah as the equal of Mary, but later Muslim tradition has made her, rather than Mary, the role model for women. The outrage of the Ayatollah Khomeini that we studied is proof positive that such a tradition has been received mythically into the deepest roots of the psyche. It has been no merely rational suggestion but rather an imperative born of a profound need to make women totally devoted to the work and message of the Prophet.

Finally, our survey of recent oral cultures has shown that a sacred mythology of femininity has been alive and well in small-scale societies. The Eskimo goddess Sedna cries out for psychological interpretation as a symbol of injured femininity, while the Lakota Buffalo Maiden fits the archetype of the provident sacred female to a T. The South American mother goddesses that we examined provide further evidence of the long-standing human instinct to incorporate femaleness into the account of how the world came to be, as of how divinity cares for it. The playful African goddess Oshun expands the usual profile of the sacred female, so that the energy of youth and eros gets its due. Finally, the Rainbow Snake of traditional Australia reminds us of the close ties to animality that many long-standing oral mythologies have found in the fertility of females.

Again and again, therefore, we find that the religious mythology of womanhood has invited people to ponder the ties of women to fertility, creation, nourishment, pleasure, and, on occasion, the purity that lies beyond sexual desire. Again and again, the mythological stands apart from the historical because the mythological deals with the archetypal, the general, the abstractable that is more significant than the concrete particular. Thus the sacral mythology of womanhood has fitted no historical woman exactly. Rather, it has called all women to associate themselves with transpersonal, cosmic patterns of fertility and nourishment.

The mythological, however, has also been historical, inasmuch as it has come from the minds and hearts of individual people. Equally, it has been historical inasmuch as it has formed the minds and hearts of individual people. So, the sacred stories about women that we find in the world religions have had enormous historical influence. Indeed, if we speak about the entire historical span of human culture, nothing has compared with their power to shape how human beings have thought about their existence as female or male.

The question now is, What ought we postmodern women and men to make of this legacy? How can we who pride ourselves on rational, historical consciousness best appropriate the ancient association of femaleness with the divine fertility, the long-standing ambiguity about women's sensuality, and the other interests and worries that have worked below rational consciousness in the psychic depths?

CONTEMPORARY IMPLICATIONS

The uniqueness of our current cultural location as women and men of a postmodern age is that we can gain and maintain considerable perspective on sacred mythologies such as those that we have studied and so address this question rationally. The humbling further fact, however, is that we cannot outrun the past formation of our species. Consequently, we delude ourselves if we think that reason can fully tame the stories handed down through humanity's great religious traditions, or that those stories have lost all their power to shape how we think about being female or male.

To take the first proposition first: We can gain, and maintain, considerable perspective on sacred mythologies because we have begun to appreciate how rich, varied, and constant they have been. For example, throughout history, in every part of the globe, the stories that people have told themselves, to make their way in the cosmos, have included influential depictions of the feminine aspects of divinity. Prior to this century, adherents of most given cultural traditions could largely ignore the myths of other people. For instance, even Christians, who had sent missionaries all over the globe for hundreds of years, could content themselves with the stories of Jesus and Mary, thinking that classical Greek or traditional Hindu or typical Jewish stories had nothing to do with their understanding of God, femaleness, or maleness. Even today, Christian theology has not appropriated the implications of a truly universal offer of "salvation" (healing of human brokenness, union with God) worked through myriad different mythologies. Even today, Christian spiritual writers can discuss classics such as the *Spiritual Exercises* of Ignatius Loyola with little acknowledgment that its symbolism, however powerful, is only one of the numberless ways that divinity has encouraged women and men to mature.[1] Divinity has been much greater than any of the world religions has liked to acknowledge. The canonical stories and patterns of behavior that any higher tradition has imposed have been as limited as they have been helpful.

To stay with the Christian case (the case probably most relevant to most of my readers), how is it possible to confess the complete adequacy of Jesus—indeed the definitive character of Jesus' expression of divinity and his work for salvation—while keeping faith with the actual efficacy of perhaps less adequate symbol systems?[2] Only by introducing an unusual humility into Christian theology and spirituality. Relatedly, one can do this only by trying, kindly yet firmly, to admit the genius of a spiritual master such as Ignatius while resisting the imperialism that many of his disciples have imposed, however unwittingly.

The more we know about the patterns of salvation, which include the ways that women have been able to think of their given shares in human nature as good, the more we find that past orthodoxies have been too rigid. Religious people must oppose a godless interpretation of cultural as well as biological evolution, according to which all has been chance. But they must also oppose interpretations that do violence to the subtlety of God's work to bring peace and joy to people's hearts. For example, it is one thing to say that the way of Jesus is to lead people to poverty, suffering, and so a humility that lets God be God, the only Master of the universe. It is another thing to say or imply that riches, prosperity, and pride are always tools of Satan. Often they have been that, but sometimes God has used them for the good of either society at large or individual people. If only in the mode of disillusionment, individuals have learned saving truths from wealth, good fortune, and good reputation. When it became clear that nothing but God—the mysterious, uncapturable Other—could satisfy the human heart, and yet that this God does not despise the wealth of creation or the fruit of human hands, people the world over have sensed the delicate, sacramental balance most fully expressed for Christians in the Incarnation.

So, on the one hand, women can use the information about the past mythological presentation of female nature now pouring forth from many different academic disciplines to relativize all traditional claims to control what they ought to try to become or how they ought to think about their share in ultimate reality. On the other hand, this same information prompts the realization that no time has been free of manipulation by mythology and that probably our own time is no exception.

For example, how free are present-day women to subject their fertility, in the most comprehensive sense of the term, to rational control? When they commit themselves to motherhood, nurturing, or nonviolent ways of resolving conflicts, are they not wise to realize, with a wry grin, that their freedom is not so much greater than their grandmothers' as they might like to think? Do their own psyches, to say nothing of their culture at large, really allow them to spurn nurturing or take up aggressive, violent ways of resolving conflicts?

Usually the answer will be no, just as it was for their grandmothers. More sophisticatedly, how effective can a model of the free, self-determining woman be if those promoting it ideologically from an antireligious platform do not recognize the Promethean character of their venture? Can one create effective new mythologies, or antimythologies, mainly from a desire to escape past stories now felt to be limiting?

Suppose the depths of women's fulfillment depend on reconciliations with a mystery finally transcendent—beyond human scale. Suppose that loving one's female nature in the ways that make it whole involve accepting the fertility, indirection, association with beauty, association with blood, and the like that the myths have always spotlighted. Suppose, in a word, that the myths, however instinctive and prerational, have expressed and mediated ineluctable truths: children come out of women; women are usually smaller than men; women cannot ignore their bodies as easily as men can; women's sexual experience has an unavoidable receptivity, passivity, seconding aspect, as well as important initiatives.

Whatever qualifications one may rightly enter, these long-playing themes of mythical femininity deserve a contemporary hearing. No matter how distant from us the cultural origins of Kali and Laksmi are, we present-day women have to call them sisters. They speak for us, though of course not completely so. We are not members of a different sex, a different species of womanhood, from what they illustrate.

As always, then, the struggle is for a balanced appropriation. Just as we fight to take from the rational past what is wise and reject what is unhealthy, so we ought to fight to take from the mythological past what still reveals us to ourselves, all the while rejecting what is unhelpful. We cannot step out of the stream of the great stories that have formed our major cultures because that stream, those stories, have determined much in what "we" are.

Christian women, for example, cannot reject the mythology of Mary without putting themselves outside the pale of Christian faith. Mary is so integral to the story of the Incarnation that without her, there would be no Christianity. In virtue of her place in the story of the Incarnation, Mary is also bound to influence greatly if not determine the main lineaments of any orthodox Christian attitude toward women. The burden of the situation for faithful Christian feminists is that we have to keep saying both no and yes. We cannot deal with Mary, or other central parts of our religious heritage, as though she were an ordinary, historical figure. We have to make the reservations and qualifications consequent on discovering that myth lies at the center of her traditional significance.

Having done this, however, we find that this myth continues to be extremely powerful, all the more so because it has historical roots in the ordinary, nonmythological aspects of Jesus and Mary. The story of Mary's conception of Jesus, giving birth to Jesus, raising Jesus, and standing by Jesus's cross continues to gather together issues utterly central to women's self-understanding: openness to God, genuine fruitfulness, suffering, and more. There is no way that faithful Christian women can avoid it.

So, the argument that I find latent in the mythological wealth of the history of religions is that we grow more appreciative of our particular heritage, not less, when we inform ourselves about the overall religious mythology of women. We gain a distance, a perspective on our particular heritage, that relieves it of any burden to be revelation without qualification. Yet we also gain the realization that our particular heritage has been a wonderful effort to accomplish the task undertaken by women and men everywhere. With greater gratitude, not less, we can realize that it has told us what we most need to know: our being, our sexual nature, is a trustworthy revelation of the being, the loving nature of God.

Notes

Chapter 1: Introduction

1. Joseph R. Veneroso, "Hail, Woman Rising!" *Maryknoll*, August 1991, p. 60.

2. Mircea Eliade, "Toward a Definition of Myth," in *Mythologies*, ed. Yves Bonnefoy (Chicago: University of Chicago Press, 1991), vol. 1, p. 4.

3. Denise Lardner Carmody, *Biblical Woman* (New York: Crossroad, 1988) and *Religious Woman* (New York: Crossroad, 1991).

Chapter 2: Old Europe and Classical Greece

1. Marija Gimbutas, *The Language of the Goddess* (San Francisco: Harper & Row, 1989), p. 5.

2. Ibid., pp. xv, xix.

3. Ibid., p. 198.

4. See Alexander Marshack, *The Roots of Civilization* (New York: McGraw-Hill, 1972).

5. See Eric Voegelin, *Order and History*, vols. 2 and 3 (Baton Rouge: Louisiana State University Press, 1957).

6. Christine Downing, *The Goddess: Mythological Images of the Feminine* (New York: Crossroad, 1981), p. 73.

7. See A. W. H. Adkins, "Greek Religion," in *Historia Religionum*, ed. C. Jouco Bleeker and Geo Widengren (Leiden: E. J. Brill, 1969), vol. 1, pp. 377–441; E. R. Dodds, *The Greeks and the Irrational* (Berkeley: University of California Press, 1951); *Mythologies*, ed. Yves Bonnefoy (Chicago: University of Chicago Press, 1991), vol. 1, pp. 325–511.

. 8. Manuela Dunn Mascetti, *The Song of Eve* (New York: Simon & Schuster, 1990), p. 66.

Chapter 3: Asian Cultures

1. David R. Kinsey, *The Sword and the Flute* (Berkeley: University of California Press, 1977), pp. 90–91, drawing on the *Markandeva-purana* 87.5–23.
2. Edward Conze, *Buddhist Wisdom Books* (New York: Harper & Row, 1972), pp. 72, 102.
3. Ibid., p. 77.
4. *Sources of Japanese Tradition*, ed. Ryusaku Tsunoda, William Theodore de Bary, and Donald Keene (New York: Columbia University Press, 1964), vol. 1, p. 27.
5. John Stratton Hawley, "A Vernacular Portrait: Radha in the *Sur Sagar*," in *The Divine Consort*, ed. John Stratton Hawley and Donna Marie Wulff (Boston: Beacon Press, 1986), p. 46.
6. Jacques Gernet, *Daily Life in China* (Stanford, Calif: Stanford University Press, 1970), p. 195.
7. Stephan Beyer, *The Cult of Tara* (Berkeley: University of California Press, 1978), p. 60.
8. Wendy Doniger O'Flaherty, *Women, Androgynes, and Other Mythical Beasts* (Chicago: University of Chicago Press, 1980), p. 100.
9. Marguerite Yourcenar, *Oriental Tales* (New York: Farrar, Straus, Giroux, 1985), pp. 124–25.
10. David Kinsley, *The Goddesses' Mirror* (Albany: State University of New York Press, 1989), pp. 65–66.

Chapter 4: Near Eastern Cultures

1. Diane Wolkstein and Samuel Noel Kramer, *Inanna* (New York: Harper & Row, 1983), pp. 108–9.
2. See Gerda Lerner, *The Creation of Patriarchy* (New York: Oxford University Press, 1986).
3. For an interpretation of the place of Greek philosophy in the history of humanity's religious development, based on the work of Eric Voegelin, see Denise Lardner Carmody and John Tully Carmody, *Interpreting the Religious Experience* (Englewood Cliffs, N.J.: Prentice-Hall, 1987), especially pp. 86–102.
4. C. J. Bleeker, "Isis and Hathor, Two Ancient Egyptian Goddesses," in *The Book of the Goddess*, ed. Carl Olsen (New York: Crossroad, 1983), pp. 32–33.
5. Pheme Perkins, "Sophia and the Mother-Father: The Gnostic Goddess," in *The Book of the Goddess*, p. 99.
6. Ibid., p. 107.
7. "Lilith," in *Encyclopaedia Judaica* (Jerusalem: Keter, 1972), vol. 11, p. 246. See also Judith Plaskow, "The Coming of Lilith: Toward a Feminist

Theology," in *Womanspirit Rising* (San Francisco: Harper & Row, 1979), pp. 198–209.

8. "Shekhinah," in *Encyclopaedia Judaica*, vol. 14, p. 1353.

9. Ibid., p. 1354.

10. Julian of Norwich, *Showings* (New York: Paulist, 1978), pp. 294–99.

11. See Carolyn Walker Bynum, *Jesus as Mother* (Berkeley: University of California Press, 1982).

12. Marina Warner, *Alone of All Her Sex* (New York: Alfred A. Knopf, 1976), pp. 335–36.

13. A. J. Aberry, trans., *The Koran Interpreted* (New York: Macmillan, 1956), vol. 1, p. 78.

14. N. J. Dawood, trans., *The Koran* (Baltimore: Penguin, 1968), pp. 33–34.

15. This paragraph first appeared in my book *The Good Alliance: Feminism, Religion, and Education* (Lanham, Md.: University Press of America, 1991), p. 63.

16. Cyril Glasse, *The Concise Encyclopedia of Islam* (San Francisco: Harper & Row, 1989), p. 123.

Chapter 5: Recent Oral Cultures

1. I have adapted this account from Denise Lardner Carmody and John Tully Carmody, *Ways to the Center*, 3d ed. (Belmont, Calif.: Wadsworth, 1989), pp. 50–51. It depends on Franz Boas, *The Central Eskimo* (Lincoln: University of Nebraska Press, 1964), pp. 175–79.

2. I have adapted these paragraphs from Denise Lardner Carmody and John Tully Carmody, *The Story of World Religions* (Mountain View, Calif.: Mayfield, 1988), pp. 62–64. They are based on Black Elk, *The Sacred Pipe*, ed. Joseph Epes Brown (Baltimore: Penguin, 1972).

3. Otto Zerries, "South American Religions: An Overview," in *Encyclopedia of Religion*, ed. Mircea Eliade (New York: Macmillan, 1987), vol. 13, p. 491.

4. I have adapted this portrait of Oshun from Joseph M. Murphy, "Oshun the Dancer," in *The Book of the Goddess*, ed. Carl Olsen (New York: Crossroad, 1983), pp. 193–94.

5. Catherine H. Berndt, "Rainbow Snake," in *Encyclopedia of Religion*, vol. 12, p. 206.

6. See A. R. Radcliffe-Brown, "The Rainbow Serpent Myth in South-East Australia," *Oceania* 7 (1930): 342–47.

Chapter 6: Conclusion

1. See, for example, William A. Barry, *Finding God in All Things* (Notre Dame, Ind: Ave Maria Press, 1991). This is a helpful exposition of the *Spiritual Exercises*, but it ignores the issue of other symbol systems, both Christian and non-Christian. In other words, it does not make foundational the point that,

though amazingly effective, the *Exercises* are merely *one* way of finding God. Any spirituality that does not make that point foundational is unfaithful to the reality of God's actual dealings with humankind.

2. See John Tully Carmody and Denise Lardner Carmody, *Christian Uniqueness and Catholic Spirituality* (New York: Paulist, 1990) and *Catholic Spirituality and the History of Religions* (New York: Paulist, 1992).